HARLEY AND DAVIDSON
FAMILY RECIPES

HARLEY AND DAVIDSON FAMILY RECIPES

Celebrating 100 Years of Home Cooking

Margo Manning
and
Carol Lange

TEN SPEED PRESS
Berkeley | Toronto

Ten Speed Press
P.O. Box 7123
Berkeley, California 94707
www.tenspeed.com

Distributed in Australia by Simon & Schuster Australia, in Canada by Ten Speed Press Canada, in New Zealand by Southern Publishers Group, in South Africa by Real Books, and in the United Kingdom and Europe by Airlift Book Company.

Designed and produced by Kate Hawley
Illustrations on pages 2, 3, 24, 50, and 138 copyright © 2003 by Pamela Scesniak
Front cover photo of William A. Davidson, in the sidecar, and William S. Harley
Back cover photo of Walter Davidson, left, and William S. Harley, right

Originally published as *Celebrating 100 Years of Genuine Harley and Davidson Family Recipes* (ISBN 0-9744406-0-4) by the William S. Harley Family History Project, Box 269, 544 East Ogden Avenue, Suite 700, Milwaukee, WI 53202-2567, wmharley1903@aol.com.

Library of Congress Control Number: 2003110896
ISBN 1-58008-622-5

First printing this edition, 2004
Printed in Canada

1 2 3 4 5 6 7 8 9 10 — 08 07 06 05 04

Dedication

"A mother is a person who, seeing there are only four pieces of pie for five people, promptly announces she never did care for pie."
—Tenneva Jordan

Carol and Margo dedicate this
collection of recipes to their mothers:

Marion "Midge" Davidson
and
Ann Mary Harley

Contents

Harley Family Tree

(partial)

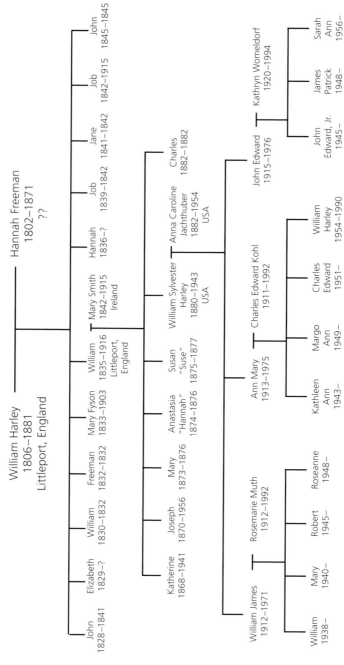

Davidson Family Tree

(partial)

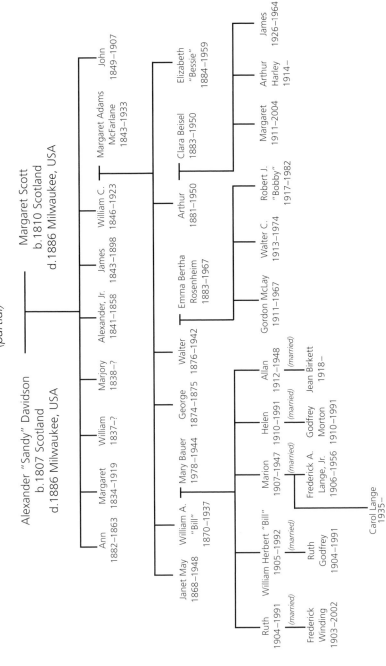

Alexander "Sandy" Davidson
b.1807 Scotland
d.1886 Milwaukee, USA

Margaret Scott
b.1810 Scotland
d.1886 Milwaukee, USA

- Ann 1882–1863
- Margaret 1834–1919
- William 1837–?
- Marjory 1838–?
- Alexander, Jr. 1841–1858
- James 1843–1898
- William C. 1846–1923
- John 1849–1907

Margaret Adams McFarlane 1843–1933

- Janet May 1868–1948
- William A. "Bill" 1870–1937 — Mary Bauer 1978–1944
- George 1874–1875
- Walter 1876–1942 — Emma Bertha Rosenheim 1883–1967
- Arthur 1881–1950 — Clara Beisel 1883–1950
- Elizabeth "Bessie" 1884–1959

Children of Walter & Emma Bertha Rosenheim:
- Gordon McLay 1911–1967
- Walter C. 1913–1974
- Robert J. "Bobby" 1917–1982

Children of Arthur & Clara Beisel:
- Margaret 1911–2004
- Arthur Harley 1914–
- James 1926–1964

Children of William A. "Bill" & Mary Bauer:
- Ruth 1904–1991 *(married)* Frederick Winding 1903–2002
- William Herbert "Bill" 1905–1992 *(married)* Ruth Godfrey 1904–1991
- Marion 1907–1947 *(married)* Frederick A. Lange, Jr. 1906–1956
- Helen 1910–1991 *(married)* Godfrey Morton 1910–1991
- Allan 1912–1948 *(married)* Jean Birkett 1918–

Carol Lange 1935–
- Jeffrey Davidson 1966–
- John David 1968–

ix

Arthur Davidson, left, and his life-long friend William S. Harley, right, playing cards with their friends. At the dawn of the twentieth century, many were drawn to the newly refined and developing internal combustion engine. The possibilities, yet to be discovered, could only be imagined. With only two years of high school education, Art and Bill were determined to "get in the game."

Introduction

"The best mirror is an old friend."
—Proverb

One hundred years ago, two best friends, William S. Harley and Arthur Davidson, became intrigued with the gas-propelled engine. At the time, they could only imagine the endless possibilities it offered. After Bill and Art assembled the first Harley-Davidson prototype, they enlisted the help of Arthur's brother Walter. Later, in 1907, William Davidson joined his brothers and Bill Harley in their budding enterprise. Since its beginning, this company was a family affair. Margaret Davidson fed her sons and their friend Bill as they worked out in the shed behind her house. Janet Davidson, their sister, named the company when she painted "Harley-Davidson Motor Company" on the door.

The company was wildly successful. Our families grew and stayed close. And we celebrated. Our cookbook aims to be part of that celebration. In the past one hundred years, Harley-Davidson's founders married, and their children and grandchildren grew up together. One of the things we've done together is cook and share our favorite foods with each other. This cookbook is a way to honor that tradition and tell a few family stories along the way. We hope you enjoy using the recipes as much as we've enjoyed discovering them.

Keep your motors running!

—Margo (Harley) Manning and Carol (Davidson) Lange

In 1895, Edward Joel Pennington came to Milwaukee to demonstrate his "motorized bicycle." In a great white plume of exhaust, he whizzed down Wisconsin Avenue, turned the "motor bicycle" around, and sputtered back. That was it! Bill Harley and Art Davidson might have witnessed Pennington that summer day, if they were in the crowd. The two best friends, only fifteen and fourteen years old, must have been enraptured. This was by far the most amazing and exciting spectacle they had ever seen.

William A. Davidson, standing, and William S. Harley, on the saddle, in a much-loved publicity photo. Both men really did enjoy fishing!

Kick Starters

As young men, during their free time, Margo's grandfather, William S. Harley, and Carol's grandfather, William A. Davidson, along with Arthur and Walter Davidson, would grab some fishing gear, pedal their bicycles, and head out to their favorite fishing spot. Legend has it that in order "to take the work out of bicycling" Bill Harley and Art Davidson began to develop their version of the motorcycle. From the very beginning, the intent of Bill Harley, Art, and Art's two brothers was to produce the best motorcycle available to the consumer. Their competition was tough.

Eventually, the Harley-Davidson motorcycle was developed, and in a short period of time it became one of the most trusted products on the market. "Taking the work out of bicycling" was an unintended secondary benefit. As time went on, because of his many other inventions for the company, Bill Harley took the work out of motorcycling, too!

William S. Harley's parents and his first-born son: Mary Smith Harley, William Harley, and baby William James Harley, who became H-D's second Chief Engineer, following in his father's footsteps

BLEICHSELLERIE MIT ROQUEFORTKÄSE

Celery with Roquefort Cheese

Margo and her cousin John Harley have been researching the Harley family roots for a number of years. They located Harley family relatives in Littleport, England.

With additional research, Margo located relatives of their grandmother. A short distance north of Munich, she found relatives of Anna Caroline Jachthuber Harley. Margo traced back to the mid-1800s, finding two brothers, Karl and Josef Jachthuber. Around 1840, Josef and his wife, Magdelena, immigrated to the United States. Karl stayed behind in Bavaria (now part of Germany). Hans Jachthuber is Karl's great-grandson. In November 2001, Margo visited with Hans and his wife, Brigitte, and other family members

Margo's mom, Ann Harley, always served this as an appetizer or on the relish tray. Little did she know at the time that she was using a Bavarian recipe! Roquefort is creamy-rich in texture with a sharp or strong flavor. It is produced from sheep's milk that is introduced to *Penicillium roqueforti*, a harmless mold, and then it is aged for three months in the limestone caverns near the village of Roquefort, in southwestern France. Always noticeable in Roquefort cheese are the blue veins the mold causes. The following recipe can be doubled or tripled for however many guests you expect. It is so easy and very delicious!

2 *stalks of celery*
4 *tablespoons butter, softened*

8 *tablespoons Roquefort cheese,*
   softened
Salt and paprika to taste

Wash and scrape the celery. Cut into 2-inch lengths. Cream the butter and mix well with the cheese. Add salt and paprika to taste. Spread the mixture in the celery hollows and serve. Serves 4.

BAKED GARLIC APPETIZER

"A nickel will get you on the subway, but garlic will get you a seat."
—Old New York Yiddish saying

2 *whole heads of garlic*
1 *tablespoon olive oil*

French bread, sliced
Goat cheese or your favorite mild
white cheese

With a very sharp knife, cut off the top of each garlic head. Pour half of the olive oil over the top of each bulb, making certain that it is absorbed between the cloves. Repeat with the remaining oil.

Preheat the oven to 375°F. In a heavy-duty covered pan or a garlic-baking dish, bake for 1 hour, or until the garlic is browned and soft. Remove from the oven. Serve with a slender knife that can scoop out the garlic to spread on the bread with some cheese.

SMOKED SALMON ROLL

1 *8-ounce package cream cheese*
(not non- or low-fat)
3 *tablespoons sour cream*

1 *2-ounce jar red caviar*
½ pound thinly sliced smoked
salmon

Bring the cream cheese to room temperature and blend with the sour cream. Gently fold in the caviar. Spread the salmon slices with the cream cheese mixture. Roll up and cut into 1½-inch lengths. Secure with a toothpick. Serve chilled.

Walter Davidson, left, and William S. Davidson, right, cruisin' down a country road.

The popularity of Harley-Davidson continued to grow. The "original factory"—the shed—could no longer accommodate the burgeoning needs of the company to produce more motorcycles. By 1907, the Harley-Davidson Motor Company moved into a new, larger wooden structure, which had an added second story.

CHEESE COOKIES FOR COCKTAILS

This original recipe is from Carol's aunt Helen Davidson-Morton, daughter of William A. Davidson, cofounder of the Harley-Davidson Motor Company.

1 *stick butter (do not use anything but real butter!)*
8 *ounces sharp cheddar cheese*
1 *cup flour*

Dash of Worcestershire sauce
Salt and pepper
2 *cups crushed Rice Krispies*

Preheat the oven to 350°F. Blend the butter, cheese, flour, Worcestershire, salt, and pepper together. Divide the Rice Krispies into 4 parts. Make nickel-sized pieces of dough and press flat into the Rice Krispies. Bake for approximately 20 minutes, or until lightly browned and crisp. Cool. The cookies can be kept in a cookie tin or frozen and reheated.

EASY AND ELEGANT MARINATED GOAT CHEESE

Fresh herbs from the farmers' market or your local grocery store make ordinary goat cheese into an elegant appetizer! Margo uses this recipe for all kinds of occasions and serves it with a variety of interesting rustic breads and assorted crackers.

1 *10-inch log of goat cheese*
1 *sprig each fresh rosemary, thyme, and marjoram*
1 *teaspoon red, green, and black peppercorns, crushed*

2 *cups olive oil*
2 *fresh bay leaves*
2 *cloves garlic, mashed and minced*
1 *teaspoon coriander seeds*

Cut the cheese into 5 separate rounds. Place the rosemary, thyme, marjoram, and peppercorns in a food processor and pulverize. Roll the edges of the goat cheese rounds in the herbs and gently press the herbs into place. Place the rounds in a container that has a tight-fitting lid. Combine the olive oil, bay leaves, garlic, and coriander seeds. Pour over the herbed goat cheese rounds. Cover and refrigerate for 2 days. Remove the cheese from the marinade and serve with crackers or bread.

PINE CONES

This holiday hors d'oeuvre recipe has been handed down in Carol's family for over twenty-five years. Along the way, Carol gave it her own special touch. Pine cones are very decorative and a special treat during the holidays.

1¼ *cups whole natural almonds*
1 *8-ounce package cream cheese*
  (not low-fat), softened
½ *cup real mayonnaise*

5 *bacon slices, cooked crispy and*
  crumbled
1 *tablespoon chopped green onion*
½ *teaspoon dill weed*
Dried pepper to taste

Toast the almonds at 300°F for 15 minutes in a shallow pan, stirring often, until they just begin to turn color. Combine the cream cheese and mayonnaise. Mix well. Add the bacon, onion, dill weed, and pepper. Cover and chill overnight. Form the cheese mixture into two pine cones, oblong in shape, narrower at tip, and wider at the bottom. Beginning at the narrow end (tip), press the almonds at slight angles into the cheese mixture in rows. Continue making overlapping rows until all the cheese mixture is covered. Garnish at the top with artificial pine sprigs. Serve with crackers of your choice or sliced French baguette. This is very festive looking—and tastes good, to boot. Makes 2 pine cones.

An early photo taken at the Juneau factory. At the time, the factory was state of the art. Many men in the neighborhood found jobs and liked the family atmosphere.

William S. Harley sits in the foreground, William Davidson is behind him, and Walter Davidson is behind him. Standing in the center back is Max Kobs, far left is Sherbie Becker, and brother Oscar sits on the saddle. A. Klein is second from the right. The four founders were trusted friends of many of their employees, oftentimes banding together to promote the company at endurance runs and other events.

EASY HOLIDAY PARTY APPETIZER

Brie cheese is produced in the French region of Brie, which is located north and west of Paris. It is a soft, mild cheese made from cow's milk, with a creamy interior and a white rind.

1 *wheel (about 2 pounds)*
  Brie cheese

½ to ¾ pound smoked salmon
Chopped fresh dill weed

Using nylon fishing line, cut the Brie into thirds horizontally. On the bottom layer, place a thin layer of smoked salmon followed by some dill. Place the next layer on top of the first and repeat the layering of salmon and dill. Place the top layer on the two completed layers. Cover the entire outside with dill. Wrap in plastic wrap and refrigerate overnight. To serve, slice the cheese into wedges in order to display the layering. Accompany with assorted crackers and sliced French bread.

   Hints: If the bread has to be sliced before the guests arrive, cover with a moistened cloth and an additional cover of plastic wrap. This should keep the sliced bread moist until your guests arrive. Also, different herbs can be substituted and others may be added. Try basil, chopped olives, pesto, or chopped almonds. You be the judge!

AUNTIE TELL'S EGGPLANT

1 *eggplant*
1 *to* **2** *tablespoons olive oil*

1 *onion, chopped*
Salt and pepper to taste

Puncture the eggplant several times on both sides. Place in a pan and broil on both sides until completely soft. Cut open to cool. When cool, peel off the skin and place in a bowl. Drain well. Using a pastry cutter, mash completely. Season to taste with olive oil, onion, salt, and pepper. Chill.

Serve chilled as a summer vegetable or on assorted crackers or sliced French bread.

MARY'S
FRESH TOMATO-BASIL CROSTINI

¾ *cup olive oil*
1 *tablespoon cider vinegar*
3 *large cloves garlic, minced*
2 *tablespoons minced fresh basil*
2 *tablespoons minced fresh parsley*

1 *to* **2** *plum tomatoes, seeded and*
  diced
Salt to taste
French baguette, sliced 1 inch thick

Preheat the oven to 350°F. Combine all of the ingredients except the bread and blend well. Toast the bread slices on a baking sheet for 10 to 15 minutes, or until nicely toasted and crisp. Serve the tomato-basil mixture in a small serving bowl surrounded by the toasted French bread slices.

ESTELLE'S SPECIAL LIVER PATÉ

Estelle was Carol's wonderful sister-in-law from California. She was a marvelous cook with a great sense of humor and the absolute best recipes.

3 *pounds chicken livers*
2 *medium onions, sliced*

Schmaltz (rendered chicken fat)
or olive oil
2 *hard-boiled eggs (optional)*

Broil the chicken livers until firm, turning frequently. When cool, put through a meat grinder or food processor until crumbled. Sauté the onions in schmaltz. Put the onions through the meat grinder. In a bowl, thoroughly mix the chicken livers and onions, adding enough schmaltz to make the right consistency for spreading; too much schmaltz will make the spread too greasy. When chilled, the mixture will thicken. It will keep in the freezer for up to 3 weeks. Decorate the top with finely chopped hard-boiled egg. Serve with assorted crackers or sliced French bread.

By 1911, the factory had changed again. It expanded into a new brick building. During the early years, the office staff and founding families gathered together not only for group photos but also for company sponsored parties. Seventh from the right is Arthur Davidson.

WISCONSIN ORANGE-CRANBERRY HOLIDAY RELISH

Make this relish at least 2 weeks ahead. This recipe is a Davidson family tradition and is always on the menu at Carol's Thanksgiving table. *Hints:* Are your cranberries fresh? Drop a few on the counter and if they bounce you know they are fresh. Add 1 teaspoon of butter to each pound of cranberries when cooking to eliminate foam and over-boiling. Cook the cranberries just until they pop; further cooking makes them taste bitter.

3 *pounds fresh cranberries*
1 *large navel orange*
1 *lime*
3 *cups white sugar*
1 *tablespoon grated fresh ginger*

1 *cup dark raisins*
2 *3-inch cinnamon sticks*
1 *vanilla bean*
Dry hot chili pepper or several
   dashes of Tabasco sauce

Wash and pick over the cranberries. Cut the orange and lime into ¼-inch slices, then dice, including the rinds. Cook the sugar in a heavy skillet over medium heat until golden. Be careful not to burn. Cool. Then stir in the diced orange, lime, ginger, raisins, cinnamon, vanilla bean, and chili pepper. Cook over high for 5 minutes, stirring continually, until thickened. Place in an airtight container and store in the refrigerator for 2 weeks. Remove the cinnamon sticks and vanilla bean, place in a relish bowl, and serve chilled.

WORLD'S GREATEST GUACAMOLE

Depending on the size of the avocados, this recipe will yield approximately a cup and a half of guacamole. Ingredients can be scaled to fit the volume of guacamole desired.

⅓ *white onion, finely chopped*
⅓ *tomato, finely chopped*
3 *ripe avocados, mashed*
3 *cloves garlic, minced*
Juice of 1 lime

Tabasco sauce (green or red or both) to taste
Worcestershire sauce to taste
Salsa of your choice to taste
Seasoning salt or plain salt to taste
Pepper to taste

Combine the onions and tomatoes and set aside. In a separate bowl, combine the avocados, garlic, and lime juice and mash with a fork to a creamy consistency. Add the Tabasco, Worcestershire, salsa, salt, and pepper to taste. Serve with corn tortilla chips and your favorite beer—but don't tell your friends how you made the guacamole. Enjoy!

MANGO SALSA

This salsa is really delicious with grilled fish and chicken.

2 *cups diced mango*
1½ *cup diced kiwi*
¾ *cup fresh corn kernels or thawed frozen corn*
½ *cup diced red onion*

½ *cup finely chopped cilantro*
3 *tablespoons fresh lime juice*
Salt and black pepper to taste
Pinch of cayenne (optional)

In a small bowl, combine all of the ingredients. Cover and chill overnight. Makes about 4 cups.

PICKLED SHRIMP APPETIZER

Shrimp are in season from May to October. When Margo lived in Alabama, the Gulf Coast city of Bayou La Batre was well known as the seafood capital of the state. Some of the best shrimp come from this quaint little city. If you want a wonderful experience, take a detour and visit this interesting coastal town.

The traditional way to cook shrimp is with the heads and shells on. Most shrimp found in grocery stores are frozen immediately when caught and then thawed for sale. From then on, the shrimp are only good for a couple days. Most shrimp that are frozen will not peel easily and have the back vein intact. Always remove an intact back vein before eating. Never defrost frozen shrimp in the microwave or at room temperature. To defrost shrimp, place in a bowl in cold water, add some ice cubes, and put in the refrigerator until completely thawed. Shrimp should always be cooked quickly in order to preserve flavor and tenderness. Cook shrimp in 3 minutes or less.

This is Carol's recipe and, as you will read below, she suggests using kosher salt.

½ cup olive oil
¼ cup red wine vinegar
½ cup fresh lemon juice
2 cloves garlic, peeled and quartered
1 medium onion, diced
½ teaspoon dry mustard

3 small bay leaves
1 teaspoon kosher salt
¼ teaspoon ground black pepper
1 pound shrimp, cooked and
   deveined*

In a glass mixing bowl, combine all of the ingredients except for the shrimp and mix well. Add the shrimp, cover, and refrigerate for 3 days. Serve with your favorite dipping sauce.

* One pound of raw shrimp in their shells equals about ½ pound of cooked and peeled shrimp.

CHILLED WATERMELON SALAD
WITH FETA CHEESE & BLACK OLIVES

Watermelon is a popular summer melon. Margo has many childhood memories of sitting on the porch at Beaver Lake on a hot summer day and devouring ice-cold, sweet summer watermelon. What could be more refreshing? An English friend of Margo's prepared this unusual combination, the centerpiece of which is watermelon. The sweet melon, creamy feta, and salty olives blended with the nutty flavor of the watercress is exceptional. If you want, the hot sauce can be eliminated from the recipe until you become more adventurous! For an even more interesting presentation, use yellow and red watermelon together.

1 *cup extra virgin olive oil*
1½ *tablespoons fresh lemon juice*
½ *teaspoon hot sauce*
Salt and freshly ground pepper to
taste
1½ *pounds seedless watermelon,*
rind removed and sliced about
¼ inch thick

½ *small red onion, sliced thinly*
¼ *cup coarsely chopped flat-leaf*
parsley or cilantro
¼ *cup pitted oil-cured black olives,*
chop coarsely
½ *cup crumbled feta cheese*
1 *bunch watercress, stemmed,*
cleaned, and dried

In a small bowl, whisk the olive oil with the lemon juice and hot sauce. Lightly salt and pepper to taste. Arrange the watermelon slices on a platter and sprinkle with the onion, parsley, olives, and feta. Evenly drizzle the dressing on top and serve over the watercress. Serves 4.

  The Jachthuber family in Germany.

BAYERISCHER ROTE RÜBE GESCHMACK

Bavarian Beet Relish

Here is another wonderful Bavarian recipe from Hans and Brigitte Jachthuber. The name Jachthuber may sound unusual to Americans, however, it dates back to feudal times in Germany. It is typical in the German language to make compound words. A "hube" was a 120-acre tract of land and, in feudal times, land was owned by a sovereign. A "huber" was a person of lower stature than the sovereign who was allowed work the land. "Jacht" means hunter, and thus, "jacht" combined with "hube" means a person who is allowed to hunt smaller game that does not interest the sovereign.

1 *tablespoon oil*
2½ *pounds beets, cooked and diced*
4 *cups finely chopped white*
   cabbage
1 *cup seeded and diced*
   sweet red pepper

1 *cup diced onion*
1½ *cups sugar*
3 *cups white vinegar*
1 *tablespoon prepared horseradish*
Salt and pepper to taste

In a heavy saucepan, heat the oil over moderately high heat until hot but not smoking. Sauté the beets, cabbage, red pepper, onion, sugar, vinegar, and horseradish. Cover and simmer, stirring occasionally, for 20 minutes. Transfer the relish to a heatproof bowl and cool. Add salt and pepper to taste. Cover and chill for at least 4 hours or up to 1 week. This relish is a wonderful accompaniment with pork and beef. It is also nice when served with assorted crackers or sliced French bread.

First and Foremost, Ladies, Start Your Engines

By the time Bill Harley and Art Davidson graduated from high school in 1898, early credible versions of the motorcycle had already been developed. Our family lore says that since their late teens, Bill Harley and Art Davidson were completely fascinated with the idea that an engine could be mounted in a bicycle frame and enthralled with the capabilities of that new machine.

In a backyard shed at the Davidson home, Bill Harley and Art Davidson began work on the first Harley-Davidson motorcycle. Art's mother, Margaret, and Bill Harley's mother, Mary, were also very good friends. The two women would cook comfort food to feed the hungry, young backyard mechanics as they began working their long hours of discovery.

Members of the office staff. Elizabeth Durr was offered a starting salary of $50 a month. In a recent interview Elizabeth recalled, "I held out for more and received $60 a month!"

MOTHER'S WILD RICE SOUP

2 *cans cream of potato soup*
2 *cups water*
1 *4-ounce can mushrooms with*
  the juice

3 *cups cooked wild rice*
1 *pound bacon, browned and diced*
1 *large onion, chopped and sautéed*
  in some bacon grease

Combine the soup, water, and mushrooms and stir until blended well. Add the rice, bacon, and onion and stir until blended well. Heat but do not boil. Serve with your favorite grated cheese. Serves 4 to 6.

JOSEPHINE SIMPSON'S ZUCCHINI SOUP

3 *tablespoons chopped onion*
3 *to* **4** *medium zucchini, washed*
  and sliced
1 *teaspoon Italian herbs or*
  garlic-and-herb seasoning

3 *to* **4** *cups chicken broth*
1 *8-ounce package cream cheese,*
  softened
Juice of 1 lemon
Salt and pepper to taste

Simmer the onion, zucchini, and herbs in the broth for about 15 minutes, or until tender. In a food processor, blend with the cream cheese in batches. Add the lemon juice and salt and pepper to taste. Couldn't be much easier!

MARGO'S FAVORITE
ROASTED RED BELL PEPPER SOUP

Everyone who tries this soup wants the recipe. It is not only delicious but very healthy, too! Since this recipe uses a lot of garlic, here are some tips on this wonderful "spice." The best garlic comes from big, firm heads with outer skins that are fine and paper-like. Garlic bulbs should be stored in a dark, dry location. Intact garlic bulbs will keep for a few months, but cloves separated from the bulb will keep for only a few days. Preserve garlic cloves that have been separated from the main bulb by placing them in a jar with enough olive oil to cover them. Cover the jar and store in the refrigerator. This method preserves the garlic cloves for a few months, and the olive oil is nicely flavored, too.

5 *large red bell peppers*
¼ *cup olive oil*
1 *large onion, chopped*
¼ *cup peeled garlic cloves*
2 *medium potatoes, peeled and*
  chopped

10 *cups low-fat, low-sodium*
  chicken broth
¼ *teaspoon ground white pepper*
¼ *teaspoon Hungarian paprika*
Salt to taste
Crème fraiche or sour cream
Snipped fresh chives

Roast the red bell peppers, then seed, remove the skin, and chop. Place the olive oil in a large soup pot over high heat and add the onion, garlic, and roasted peppers. Sauté for about 5 minutes, or until the onion and garlic are lightly browned, stirring frequently. Add the potatoes, chicken stock, white pepper, and paprika. Bring to a boil, then simmer, uncovered, for about 30 minutes, or until the vegetables are soft. In small batches, ladle the soup and vegetables into a food processor. Purée on high speed until smooth and creamy. When completed, pour back into the soup pot, and season with salt to taste. Ladle the soup into soup bowls and garnish with crème fraiche and chives.

A portrait of Margo's grandmother, Anna Caroline Jachthuber Harley, during the 1920s.

Carol Lange, daughter of Marion "Midge" Davidson, at her friend Mona's party in 1950. Remember shirtwaists?

SPANISH GAZPACHO

1 *46-ounce can tomato juice*
5 *large tomatoes, cut into pieces*
  with skins
2 *large cloves of garlic, crushed*
¼ *to* ½ *cup good-quality olive oil*
1 *teaspoon salt*
1 *to* **2** *tablespoons white vinegar*
¼ *cup or more bread crumbs*
  (to thicken)
Pinch of sugar

Toppings
Chopped tomatoes
½ *red onion, chopped*
Cucumber, seeded and chopped
Croutons (optional)
Diced green pepper (optional)

Put the tomato juice and tomatoes in a blender and blend well. Add the garlic, olive oil, salt, vinegar, bread crumbs, and sugar and blend again. Ladle into bowls and top with chopped tomatoes, onion, cucumber, croutons, and green pepper. Serve.

CAROL'S BLACK BEAN SOUP

1 *pound dried black beans*
2 *bacon slices, cut into ½-inch*
  pieces
1 *cup chopped onion*
1 *teaspoon dried thyme*
3 *cloves garlic, minced*
2 *bay leaves*
5 *cups chicken stock*
3 *cups water*
½ *teaspoon salt*

Toppings
Corn tortillas, cut into strips
Chopped onion
Minced cilantro
Lime wedges
Andouille sausage

Rinse and pick over the dried beans. Cover with water 2 inches above the beans and bring to a boil. Cook for 2 minutes. Remove from the heat. Cover and let stand for 1 hour. Drain. Cook the bacon in the pan over medium heat until crisp. Remove the bacon from the pan. Add the chopped onion, thyme, garlic, and bay leaves to the bacon drippings. Sauté for 4 minutes. Add the beans, bacon, stock, and water to the pan. Bring to a boil, then decrease the heat and simmer for 1½ hours, stirring occasionally. Add the salt and simmer for another 30 minutes, or until the beans are tender. Discard the bay leaves. Purée or mash the soup to a texture you like.

Preheat the oven to 350°F. Place a single layer of the tortilla strips on a cookie sheet. Bake for 12 minutes, or until the strips are toasted. Serve the soup and sprinkle with the toppings of your choice.

During the 1930s and 1940s, Cuba was a favorite vacation spot. This picture shows Carol's mother, Marion Davidson Lange, on the porch of a hotel.

BAYRISCHE LEBERKNOEDELSUPPE

Bavarian Liver Dumpling Soup

Stock
8 *ounces stewing meat, marrow,*
  or chicken bones
5 *cups water*
1 *small onion, chopped*
2 *stalks celery, chopped*
2 *carrots, peeled and chopped*
Salt and pepper to taste

Dumplings
6 *stale crusty rolls, thinly sliced*
Milk
1 *egg, beaten*
4 *ounces liver, diced*
1 *tablespoon diced onion*
1 *tablespoon minced parsley*
2 *slices bacon, cooked and*
  crumbled
Pinch of salt
⅛ *teaspoon marjoram*
Chopped chives

To make the stock, place the meat in a stewing pot with the water. Cover and boil for about 1 hour. Add the chopped vegetables and cook for another 45 minutes. Season with salt and pepper and strain, reserving only the stock.

To make the dumplings, soak the bread crusts in some milk and then squeeze out all of the liquid. Mince the soaked bread and all of the other ingredients exept the chives until they form a paste. Form into teaspoon-sized balls and drop gently into the boiling stock. Simmer for 10 minutes. Garnish with chopped chives. Serves 4 to 6.

POLISH CABBAGE SALAD

Salata Z Kapusty

This recipe comes from a college friend of Carol's. It is one of those great recipes that comes together quickly and has a number of simple but different and interesting flavors.

Here are a few helpful hints for cooking with cabbage: One pound of cabbage equals 4 cups of shredded cabbage or 2 cups of cooked cabbage. Look for compact heads that are heavy for their size. The cabbage head should be unblemished and not curling. The fastest way to remove the outer leaves in one piece is to cut around the base of the core. Gently remove the core and loosen each leaf at its base.

4 *cups shredded cabbage*
1 *teaspoon salt*
1 *tablespoon fresh lemon juice*

½ *teaspoon dill seed*
1 *tablespoon powdered sugar*
2 *teaspoons olive oil*

Mix the cabbage, salt, and lemon juice together and let stand for 4 hours. Stir the dill seed, powdered sugar, and olive oil into the cabbage. Toss lightly. Serves 4 to 6.

AUNT HELEN DAVIDSON'S
LEGACY GARLIC SALAD

In Milwaukee's *Exclusively Yours* magazine (April 1958), Kathy French wrote, "Fortunate is the man who has married a good cook—until she decides to write a cookbook." The article referred to Helen Davidson Morton and her childhood friend Ellen Whyte Stolz. Helen and Ellen wrote their cookbook in the third-floor studio of Helen's home in Elm Grove, Wisconsin. Published in 1956, their cookbook was titled *Choice Family Recipes.*

This recipe from Aunt Helen was not included in her cookbook. Carol's two sons, Jeff and John, both devour this salad, and it has also become their choice family favorite!

Here are some interesting olive oil facts! The olive branch is a symbol of peace. Olive trees, if properly cultivated, can have a lifespan of three to seven hundred years. The use of olive oil dates back to ancient Greece. To the ancients, the olive became a symbol of prosperity. The olive was cultivated and its oil was used for cooking and as fuel for oil-burning lamps.

Always cook with the best olive oil available. A lesser-grade olive oil leaves a distinct aftertaste. Conduct a "taste test" and compare the pure, the extra virgin, and the premium extra virgin. There is a huge difference that will influence the success of a recipe. Store olive oil in a cool location in an airtight glass, porcelain, or stainless-steel container. Never use plastic containers; PVCs are easily absorbed into any oil, especially olive oil.

1 *head of iceberg lettuce, washed and broken into pieces by hand*
2 *cloves fresh garlic, mashed into the bottom of a salad bowl*

4 *tablespoons good quality olive oil*
2 *tablespoons white distilled vinegar*
Salt to taste

Add the lettuce to the bowl with the mashed garlic. Coat well by tossing with the olive oil. Add the vinegar and toss. Add salt to taste. If you use decide to use half a head of lettuce, also cut the oil, vinegar, and garlic in half. Serve immediately.

Helen Davidson Morton, daughter of William A. Davidson, is Carol's dear aunt. Aunt Helen penned the very first family cookbook titled Choice Family Recipes, which became a huge success. As authors of the second family cookbook, we owe her a great debt of gratitude for her foresight and creativity.

Davidson sisters visiting New Orleans in 1948. Ruth Davidson Winding, left, and Helen Davidson Morton, right, daughters of William A. Davidson

JO BOBBY'S CREAMY SALAD DRESSING

Jo Bobby, otherwise known as Charlotte Gafford, is the mother of Margo's best friend, Charlotte. When Charlotte and her husband, George, moved to the country a few miles southwest of Nashville, Tennessee, everyone received their "country name." Charlotte's mom became "Jo Bobby." Jo Bobby was one of the most interesting women I ever had the pleasure to meet. She enjoyed an occasional cigarette, a very dry martini, exquisite food, and, if delicious, some gossip. All of us loved her so much and miss her dearly.

½ teaspoon ground white pepper
¼ teaspoon salt
4 teaspoons white wine vinegar

5 tablespoons heavy cream
5 tablespoons peanut oil or corn oil

Combine the pepper, salt, vinegar, and cream and beat until well blended. Add the oil and stir until blended. Serve on any combination of fresh washed greens.

SESAME SEED SALAD DRESSING

After college graduation, Carol attended cooking classes in Hawaii, and it was there she learned this tip for peeling garlic. Position a clove of garlic in the center of a your cutting board. With the flat side of a chef knife or cleaver on top of the garlic, swiftly push down using the heel of your hand to break the outer skin. Simply remove the outer skin.

2 to 3 tablespoons sesame seeds
⅓ cup water
⅓ cup wine vinegar
½ teaspoon Worcestershire sauce
¼ teaspoon Dijon-style mustard
¼ cup sugar

½ small clove garlic, crushed and
* minced*
½ teaspoon pepper
½ teaspoon salt or less
½ cup olive oil
2 to 3 drops sesame seed oil

Toast the sesame seeds in a heavy skillet until slightly brown, watching carefully and stirring constantly. Set aside. Mix the rest of the ingredients together in a jar, adding the oil last. Just before serving, add the sesame seeds (usually 2 tablespoons per person).

TEN-MINUTE BEAN SALAD

Make this salad a few hours ahead so that it can marinate. *Warning:* Be careful handling any kind of chili peppers. Hot peppers contain oils and can burn your skin—especially your eyes! We suggest wearing rubber gloves while handling chilies, or wash your hands and nails thoroughly with soap and water after handling.

Dressing
3 *tablespoons fresh lemon juice*
1 *tablespoon olive oil*
½ *teaspoon salt*
¼ *teaspoon ground cumin*
Pinch of fresh black pepper
1 *large clove garlic, minced*

3 *15½-ounce cans beans (a combination of garbanzo, black-eyed peas, and red kidney)*
½ *cup chopped green onions including some of the green tops*
1 *3-inch fresh chili pepper, washed, seeded, and chopped*
3 *tablespoons finely chopped fresh cilantro*

To make the dressing, combine the lemon juice, olive oil, salt, cumin, black pepper, and minced garlic.

To make the salad, drain the beans well and put in a bowl. Add the chopped green onions. Add the chopped chili and cilantro. Toss the beans and dressing together and marinate for a few hours.

*Carol's grandmother, Mary Bauer Davidson, and her cousin Billie,
later known as Willie G.*

Carol's mother, Marion "Midge" Davidson Lange. Midge was well known for her famous peanut brittle recipe, which we have included in this book.

CURRIED ARTICHOKE RICE SALAD

This salad deliciously combines all of Margo's favorite ingredients. Set aside a few artichoke quarters to use on the top. If you like the taste of curry, use more!

1 *package chicken-flavored Rice-a-Roni*
1 *8-ounce jar marinated artichokes, quartered*
⅜ *cup mayonnaise*

2 *teaspoons curry powder or to taste (Margo uses a lot more!)*
6 *to* **7** *green onions, chopped*
½ *cup sliced almonds*

Cook the Rice-a-Roni according to the package's directions, but use ¼ cup less water. Cool in a large serving bowl. Drain the marinated artichokes and reserve the liquid and artichoke quarters. Combine the reserved liquid and the mayonnaise and stir until blended. (*Hint:* If the marinade is too oily, drain off some of it before mixing with the mayonnaise.) Add the curry powder. Combine the Rice-a-Roni, onions, almonds, and drained artichokes and toss. Add the dressing slowly and toss; you may not need all of it. Add the saved artichoke quarters, some more almonds, and a few diced red peppers as a decoration.

MARIA'S SPANISH SALAD WITH BARCELONA MAYONNAISE

2 *egg yolks, slightly beaten*
½ *teaspoon salt*
½ *teaspoon powdered mustard*
⅛ *teaspoon sugar*
Pinch of cayenne pepper

4 *to* **5** *teaspoons white vinegar*
1½ *cups olive oil*
4 *teaspoons hot water*
Chilled parboiled diced carrots, potatoes, peas, and green beans

Beat the yolks, salt, mustard, sugar, cayenne, and 1 teaspoon of the vinegar in a small bowl until thick and light yellow. Slowly add ¼ cup of the olive oil, beating vigorously. Beat in 1 teaspoon of the vinegar and 1 teaspoon of the hot water. Slowly add another ¼ cup of the oil, beating vigorously. Beat in 1 teaspoon of the vinegar and 1 teaspoon of the hot water. Add ½ cup of the oil in a fine stream, beating constantly, then beat in the remaining vinegar and water. Slowly beat in the remaining oil. If it's too thick, add a little hot water. Cover and refrigerate for up to 1 week. Makes about 1½ cups. Serve over the vegetables.

LOIS'S REVOLUTIONARY
SOUTHERN SPOON BREAD

Lois is Carol's friend of many years. They both enjoy cooking, entertaining, and introducing friends to their favorite recipes. Legend tells us spoon bread originated during the Revolutionary War and became a favorite of George Washington. Because of its density, it was originally served with a spoon—hence, its name. In early American history, cornmeal emerged as a highly profitable commodity for farmers across the country. Relatively inexpensive to make, Southern spoon bread (also known as corn bread) became a staple in the diet of both Union and Confederate soldiers. Civil War soldiers had to cook for themselves. Given the limited availability of ingredients, attention to a recipe was all but forgotten or impossible. This recipe works with even fewer eggs or substituting some other oil for butter. During the Civil War, most foods were fried in grease, which became a good source for stored energy (though today we consider grease unhealthy).

These days, when Margo makes spoon bread, she thinks of her great-grandfather (another William Harley), who emigrated from Littleport, England, in 1859. On February 11, 1864, he enlisted as a private in Company F of the 13th, New York Volunteer, Heavy Artillery. On July 18, 1865, he was transferred to Company L of the 6th, New York Volunteer, Heavy Artillery.

The creation of a great recipe starts with a basic recipe from the past. To this corn bread, you can add grated cheddar cheese and jalapeño peppers, Use your imagination; you be the chef!

3 *cups milk*
1¼ *cups white cornmeal (water*
   ground is best)
3 *eggs, well beaten*

2 *tablespoons butter, melted*
1¾ *teaspoon baking powder*
1 *teaspoon salt*

Preheat the oven to 350°F. Boil the milk and immediately add the cornmeal. Cook for about 5 minutes, stirring constantly, until very thick. Remove from the heat and cool until very stiff. Add the eggs, butter, baking powder, and salt. Beat with an electric beater until well blended. Pour into a well-greased casserole about 6 inches in diameter by 3 inches deep. Bake for 45 minutes, or until a knife inserted in the center comes out clean. Serve in spoonfuls!

Stella Forge and Elizabeth Durr Moyle. Stella was the receptionist for many, many years at the company. If you called, the first person you talked to was Stella. Stella never married and was a devoted employee and close friend of all the founding families. This picture comes from Elizabeth Durr Moyle, taken at one of Crystal Haydel's many parties. As you can see, Stella and Elizabeth liked to ride!

In November 2001, Margo visited Littleport, England, the ancestral home of the Harley family. Littleport is where her great-grandfather emigrated from in 1859. Located just north of Cambridge and Ely, Littleport is in the heart of the Fens. This picture, taken at the Black Horse Pub, is of the Handley family, cousins of the American Harleys. Margo is third from the right.

BEST-EVER ENGLISH SCONES

4 *cups flour, sifted*
½ *cup sugar*
2 *teaspoons cream of tartar*
1 *teaspoon baking soda*
Pinch of salt

6 *tablespoons butter*
1 *cup milk*
1 *egg*
1½ *cups raisins*

Preheat the oven to 500°F. In a large mixing bowl, combine the flour, sugar, cream of tartar, baking soda, and salt. Cut in the butter until grainy in texture. Whisk the egg and milk. Add the raisins. Add the egg-raisin mixture to the dry ingredients. Lightly flour a wooden board. Knead the dough and roll into a round about 1 inch thick. Cut into equal triangles and place on an ungreased baking sheet. Decrease the oven heat to 400°F and bake for 8 to 10 minutes.

JOHN & MARY'S PARMESAN–POPPY SEED PULL-APART BREAD

3 *tablespoons butter, melted*
1 *tablespoon minced onion, sautéed*
1 *tablespoon poppy seed*
¼ *teaspoon celery seed*

1 *10½-ounce package prepared flaky biscuits (from the grocery dairy section)*
¼ *cup grated Parmesan cheese*
1½ *teaspoons dried dill weed*

Preheat the oven to 400°F. Melt the butter in a 9-inch round pan. Sprinkle the onion, poppy seed, and celery seed over the butter. Cut each biscuit into four pieces. Put the Parmesan cheese and dill weed in a bag. One at a time, shake the four biscuit pieces in the bag and then arrange in the pan. Sprinkle the remaining cheese-dill mixture over the top. Bake for 15 to 18 minutes. Turn onto a serving platter.

GREAT-GRANDMA MARY SMITH HARLEY'S OLD COUNTRY IRISH SODA BREAD

This recipe is a breakfast treat! Make it the day before serving. Since Margo's great-grandparents lived in Wisconsin, fresh butter abounded. Serve with room-temperature butter, homemade marmalade, or your favorite jelly or jam. Nothing could be better to start off your morning breakfast. *Hint:* Do not double this recipe; make it in two batches if you have a hungry crowd!

4 *cups flour*
1½ *teaspoons salt*

1 *teaspoon baking soda*
2 *cups buttermilk*

Preheat the oven to 375°F. Grease a medium-sized baking sheet. In a large mixing bowl lightly blend the flour, salt, and baking soda. To the flour mixture, add the buttermilk and blend with a fork until the dough forms a ball. On a lightly floured board, knead the dough gently for 20 seconds. Shape into a round about 8 inches in diameter and 1½ inches thick. Using an oiled sharp knife, cut an "X" over the top about ¼ inch deep. Place the dough on a greased baking sheet and bake for about 45 to 50 minutes, or until the bread is lightly browned. Place on a rack to cool. Wrap with a slightly damp towel and let rest on the rack for at least 8 hours.

The Harley family lived at 12th and Burleigh in Milwaukee for many years. The house is no longer standing. A very young and handsome William S. Harley is the man in the middle of this picture.

On the Course and on the Trail

Not long after Bill Harley and Art, Walter, and Bill Davidson began manufacturing motorcycles full time, governments around the world began building better roads. A lot of roads! In 1903, the United States had about 2.4 million miles of road, but only 9 percent had hard surfaces. Consequently, when it rained, dirt roads became muddy and next to impossible to navigate.

The Harley-Davidson Motor Company was born during an exciting era of change. During the last two decades of the nineteenth century, curiosity about the internal combustion engine swept over the entire world. Its further development enabled most modes of transportation to advance out of the horse-and-buggy era forever. The discovery, at the turn of the century, of how to refine oil into a high-powered liquid called gasoline opened the door to the automotive age. And, Henry Ford's revolutionary assembly line in 1910 made it possible to manufacture cars in higher volume and at lower cost. There was no turning back.

William S. Harley, left, rode to the top of Pike's Peak on July 8, 1920. On the back of the photo he wrote, "At Glen Cove, just timberline elevation 12,000 feet, on way up Pike's Peak. Notice snow and ice. Yes and 'twas in July too."

FAMILY PICNIC COLESLAW

Coleslaw is a favorite Harley family picnic go-with-everything treat. Coleslaw accompanies any main course at a picnic: hot dogs, bratwurst, hamburgers, sloppy joes, spare ribs—you name it! It is best if the coleslaw is prepared and served the same day to insure that the cabbage remains crispy.

Coleslaw can be prepared with creamy or vinaigrette dressing. Ann Harley always used vinaigrette dressing. To add another dimension, whisk in ½ teaspoon minced fresh ginger and ½ cup chopped cilantro. A sprinkle of ground cayenne pepper will give it a little heat! This is also a delicious dressing with a tossed salad.

Dressing
1 to **3** teaspoons fresh lemon juice
¼ cup white balsamic vinegar
½ tablespoon Dijon-style mustard
1 clove garlic, minced and puréed
¾ cup extra virgin olive oil
Salt and pepper to taste

Vegetables
1 dense head of white cabbage, shredded (4 to 5 cups)
½ to ⅔ cups shredded carrots
¼ cup diced onion (if available, use Vidalia or Walla-Walla onions)

To prepare the dressing, combine the lemon juice, vinegar, mustard, and garlic. With a wire whisk, blend until creamy in texture. Slowly add the olive oil so that the mixture does not separate. Add salt and black pepper to taste.

To make the slaw, combine the cabbage, carrots, and onion in a large bowl. Pour the dressing over the vegetables and toss.

ENDURANCE RUN SPINACH PASTA SALAD

Pasta is a wonderful source of carbohydrates, which the body draws upon for energy. In August of 1910, Margo's grandpa, William S. Harley, won the "Endurance Run" of the Federation of American Motorcyclists. The November 30, 1910, issue of *Motorcycling* magazine records: "Getting through that first afternoon of the National F.A.M. Endurance Run, when most others died; getting up in front of the national assembly and saying his say in plain deep-voiced American; going at things generally so as to make them come his way—that is the kind of fellow Harley is."

Grandpa Harley probably didn't "carb up" before that race, but having the medal presented to him that day became a huge honor for his family. Margo has that medal tucked away: she named this salad in honor of her grandpa winning that race. It is full of interesting flavors, easy to make, and a recipe you can certainly add to. Inspiration and pasta go hand in hand. Try adding cubed chicken left over from another meal.

8 *ounces pasta (any type you prefer)*
2 *cloves garlic, crushed*
4 *tablespoons olive oil*
1½ *teaspoons balsamic vinegar*
1 *teaspoon lemon juice*
1 *teaspoon Dijon-style mustard*
½ to ¾ *pound fresh spinach, washed and coarsely chopped*

¼ *cup finely chopped red onion*
¼ *cup French oil-cured black and green olives with herbs de Provence, pitted and sliced*
4 *plum tomatoes, seeded and diced*
1 *tablespoon lightly chopped fresh basil or cilantro*
Crumbled feta cheese

In boiling salted water, cook the pasta according to the package's directions. In a colander, drain the pasta, rinse in cold water, and drain again.

In a small mixing bowl, combine the garlic, olive oil, vinegar, lemon juice, and mustard. Stir with a wire whisk until well blended.

In a large mixing bowl, combine the cooked pasta, spinach, olives, tomatoes, and basil. Toss together. Drizzle the dressing over the top and toss again. Serve with crumbled feta cheese sprinkled over the top. Serves 4 to 6.

Following a Federation of American Motorcyclists endurance race, this newspaper photo was taken. From the left: Margo's grandfather, William S. Harley; Carol's great-uncle, Walter Davidson; Frank Ollerman; and A. Klein.

"Pardon us! Can we cook a few bratwurst?" William S. Harley, left, and Anna Caroline Harley, right, enjoying a cookout in the country with some friends.

SPECIALLY DEVELOPED HAMBURGERS

This recipe comes from Carol's daughter-in-law, Mary, wife of Carol's son John.

1½ *teaspoon salt or less*
½ *teaspoon fresh ground pepper*
⅛ *teaspoon ground cayenne*
¼ *teaspoon paprika*

⅛ *teaspoon chili powder*
1 *pound ground beef*
1 *cup chopped onions*

Combine the salt, pepper, cayenne, paprika, and chili powder in a large mixing bowl. Add the ground beef and onions and thoroughly mix together. These burgers are best if cooked on the grill. Enjoy with a fresh baked roll and dress it up with sliced tomato, onion, catsup, and mustard.

FULLY DRESSED DOGS

Here are some tips for making great hot dogs: Always buy the best hot dogs, frankfurters, or wieners. To cook, boil in a combination of beer and water or grill them outdoors. Brush your hot dogs with canola oil when broiling or grilling out. The oil will give the outer skin a nice crispness. Next to olive oil, canola oil is one of the healthiest and safest oils available. It is reported to be high in monounsaturated and polyunsaturated fats, or "good" fats. Canola oil possesses a high smoking point and therefore will not burn as easy. It has a neutral, mild taste that does not overpower other flavors. Use any combination of the condiments below to dress your dog, then lean back and yowl!

Poppy seed buns
Chopped onions (red onions are best)
Pickle relish
Marinated yellow hot peppers
Tomatoes
Celery salt

Sliced cucumber
Dill pickle
Sauerkraut
Thousand Island dressing
Mustard
Pickle spears (the crowning glory)

William S. Harley standing before a Wisconsin corn field. What a beauty of a motorcycle—and the corn looks healthy, too!

WISCONSIN-STYLE CHEESE SANDWICH

5½ *ounces cheddar cheese, grated*
3 *medium egg yolks, lightly beaten*
1 *tablespoon Worcestershire sauce*
Salt and pepper to taste
6 *drops Tabasco sauce*

1 *fluid ounce dark beer*
1 *teaspoon mustard*
8 *slices of bread (try San Francisco sourdough—yummy)*

Mix all of the ingredients except for the bread together. Toast the bread on both sides. Spread the cheese mixture on top about ½ inch thick. Grill on the stove top until nicely browned. Enjoy with your favorite Milwaukee beer.

HELEN DAVIDSON MORTON'S
SOUR CREAM POTATO SALAD

This wonderful Davidson family favorite is great for a summer picnic. On the original recipe card, Aunt Helen wrote, "This is my own recipe and we think it is delicious." And so do we. Enjoy!

5 *to* **6** *good-sized new potatoes (or 12 small)*
1 *bunch green onions, finely cut*
4 *tender stalks of celery, thinly cut*
2 *tablespoons finely chopped parsley*

1 *cup sour cream*
1 *cup salad dressing*
½ *cup mayonnaise*
¼ *to* **½** *cup sweet pickle juice*
2 *tablespoons sweet pickle relish*

Cook the potatoes. Chill and then cube. Place in a large bowl, add the green onions, celery, and parsley and toss. Combine the sour cream, salad dressing, mayonnaise, pickle juice, and relish. Toss with the potato mixture. Refrigerate for 12 to 24 hours to season. Serves 4 to 8.

CALEXICO SOUR CREAM TORTILLAS

Looking for an easy recipe to serve guests who are vegetarians? Here it is! Tortilla comes from the Spanish word *torta*, meaning "round cake," and dates back thousands of years B.C. The tortilla was a staple of the native Aztecs during the sixteenth century. Today, tortillas are plentiful and available in almost every grocery store in the United States. Tortillas are as popular as bread, muffins, and bagels. A tortilla will wrap around almost any food anyone wants to eat. The possibilities are endless.

12 *large corn or flour tortillas*
1 *medium onion, chopped*
1 *tablespoon oil*
1 *20-ounce can tomatoes*
½ *cup white wine*
1 *teaspoon ground oregano*

Salt to taste
½ *cup grated Parmesan cheese*
1 *cup cubed Jack cheese*
1 *pint sour cream*
1 *cup coarsely grated cheddar cheese*

Preheat the oven to 350°F. Arrange the tortillas in the bottom of a casserole. In a skillet, sauté the onions in oil. Add the tomatoes, wine, oregano, and salt. Simmer for 15 minutes. Pour the mixture over the tortillas. Add the Parmesan cheese and Jack cheese. Spread the sour cream over all. Bake for 30 minutes. Add the cheddar cheese and bake, uncovered, for 5 to 10 minutes. Serve with salad and fruit. Serves 6.

CHICKEN FAJITAS WITH PEPPERS

¼ cup canola oil
Pinch of salt
2 tablespoons ground oregano
2 to **4** large chicken breasts,
  deboned and cubed
¼ cup vinegar
3 peppers (red, green, and yellow),
  seeded and sliced

1 red onion, sliced
4 cloves garlic
1 teaspoon cumin
¾ pound shrimp
Flour or corn tortillas
1 tablespoon olive oil
Guacamole
Sour cream

Heat half of the canola oil, the salt, and oregano in a large nonstick frying pan and cook the chicken cubes. Marinate the peppers and onion in the vinegar and olive oil. In a separate pan, heat the remaining canola oil. Add the peppers, onions, garlic, and cumin and sear. Add the shrimp in the last 2 to 3 minutes of vegetable cooking (or they will become tough). Have the tortillas ready and fill at the table or before hand. Serve with guacamole and sour cream. Serves 2 to 4.

FRESNO BAD BOY GRILLED TRI-TIP BEEF

Carol's son Jeff contributed this recipe. He lives in Fresno, California, and is a pilot for American Airlines. If you have never heard of tri-tip beef before, it is a special cut of beef. If you don't see tri-tip in the meat case, ask the butcher to order it. A beef tri-tip roast is boneless, from the bottom sirloin. It is called a "triangular" roast because of its shape. Tri-tip roasts vary from 1½ to 2 pounds and are about 2 inches thick. It is tender and delicious!

Tri-tip beef, at room temperature

Pappy's low-salt seasoning or your
  favorite seasoning salt

Stoke up your barbeque. Have a beer while waiting. Lightly coat each side of the meat with Pappy's seasoning. Refrigerate for about 30 minutes. Barbecue and enjoy.

COUSIN PEGGY'S
SLOW-COOKED BAKED BEANS

In Boston, the home of famous baked bean recipes, coleslaw is usually served with baked beans. This recipe can be doubled and tripled very easily depending upon the number of guests and how hungry they are!

1 *16-ounce can of your favorite prepared baked beans, with or without meat*
¼ *cup chopped onion*

½ *cup brown sugar*
½ *cup dark molasses*
3 *squirts catsup or to taste*

Put all of the ingredients into a crock-pot or heavy casserole, mix together, and go for a ride on your bike! This recipe can be made 1 or 2 days ahead of time. Serves 4 to 6.

SUZIE'S FAMOUS
SPINACH NOODLE CASSEROLE

6 *ounces medium noodles*
1 *10-ounce package frozen chopped spinach, thawed and drained*
1 *pint cottage cheese*
½ *cup shredded Parmesan cheese*
½ *cup shredded cheddar cheese*
½ *cup sour cream*

1 *teaspoon salt*
Dash of Tabasco sauce
¼ *teaspoon ground basil*
¼ *cup thyme*
1 *tablespoon butter, melted*
¼ *cup bread crumbs*

Preheat the oven to 350°F. Cook the noodles and drain. In a large mixing bowl, combine the spinach, cottage cheese, Parmesan cheese, cheddar cheese, sour cream, salt, Tabasco, basil, and thyme and mix well. Add the noodles and combine. Turn out into a 1½-quart casserole dish. Combine the melted butter and bread crumbs. Sprinkle over the casserole. Cover and bake for 45 minutes.

A couple out in the woods enjoying nature. However, one of them must have walked, because there is not a sidecar or buddy seat! One of the great achievements of the internal combustion engine was that it enabled an individual to do things and go places that were impossible or too difficult before. Not long after the refinement of the gas-propelled engine, local governments began building roads—lots of roads! In 1903, the United States had about 2.4 million miles of roads, but only 9 percent had hard surfaces. Consequently, when it rained, dirt roads became muddy and next to impossible to navigate with any vehicle possessing any number of wheels.

From the left: William S. Harley with his wife, Anna Caroline, enjoying a day in the country with the first Harley-Davidson dealer, C. H. Lang of Chicago, Illinois. Clara Beisel Davidson, wife of Arthur Davidson, accompanies them. Arthur was the photographer. C. H. Lang opened for business as the first Harley dealer and sold one of the first three production Harley-Davidson motorcycles ever produced.

LES'S FAMOUS CHOW-DOWN CHILI

"Whenever I meet someone who does not consider chili a favorite dish,
then I've usually found someone who has never tasted good chili."
—Jane Butel, from *Chili Madness*

Les was Margo's good friend and a coworker in the costume shop at the Milwaukee Repertory Theater. His recipes were always inventive and flavorful. He passed away a few years ago, and his talent and humor are remembered and missed by all who were lucky enough to know him.

Margo likes to use a combination of dark red kidney, lima, great northern, and pinto beans, which are all available frozen, so only what is needed can be used. *Hint:* When sautéeing onions and garlic, sauté the onions first and then add the garlic. This prevents the garlic from being overcooked and becoming bitter.

2 *pounds lean ground beef or turkey*
1 *medium onion, chopped*
1 *clove garlic, crushed and minced*
1 *tablespoon olive oil*
1 *8-ounce can tomato sauce*
1 *8-ounce can crushed tomatoes*
3 *tablespoons chili powder (or less, if you prefer)*
1 *teaspoon cinnamon*
1 *teaspoon ground cumin*

1 *teaspoon ground cloves*
⅛ *teaspoon nutmeg*
½ *cup chopped fresh cilantro*
Salt and black pepper to taste
1 *16-ounce can dark red kidney beans (or a combination of beans)*
Cooked spaghetti or other noodles
Shredded cheese (for example, sharp cheddar or mozzarella)
Sour cream

Brown the meat, drain off the excess fat, and set the meat aside. In a large cooking pot, sauté the onion and garlic in the olive oil. Add the browned meat, tomato sauce, crushed tomatoes, chili powder, cinnamon, cumin, cloves, nutmeg, and cilantro. Simmer over low heat, uncovered, for approximately 1 hour. Add salt and pepper to taste. Add the beans, stir, and cook for another 10 minutes. To serve, place some cooked spaghetti or noodles in a bowl, ladle in some chili, and top with your choice of toppings—cheese, sour cream, or both! Serves 6 to 8.

CRUISIN' CALIFORNIA CASSEROLE

White Sauce
2 *tablespoons flour*
2 *tablespoons butter*
1 *cup milk*
Salt and pepper to taste

1 *can artichoke hearts (10 hearts),*
  quartered

1½ *pounds crabmeat or shrimp*
1 *cup white sauce*
6 *mushrooms, sliced*
¼ *cup dry sherry*
1 *tablespoon Worcestershire sauce*
½ *teaspoon salt*
Pinch of pepper
¼ *cup grated Parmesan cheese*

To make the white sauce, in a small saucepan, melt the butter and stir in the flour. Cook for a few minutes. Slowly incorporate the milk. Over medium heat, stir until the sauce thickens. Add salt and pepper to taste.

To make the casserole, preheat the oven to 375°F. Layer the artichokes on the bottom of a shallow, buttered baking dish. Spread the crabmeat or shrimp on top. Combine the white sauce, mushrooms, sherry, Worcestershire, salt, and pepper and pour over the artichokes and crabmeat or shrimp. Sprinkle the cheese over the top. Bake for 25 to 30 minutes. Serves 4.

William S. Harley was an avid sportsman. Riding a motorcycle, camping, hunting, fishing, and golf were among his favorites. Arthur Davidson, Jr., was his golf caddie. Art recalled how Bill Harley used to "engineer" his own golf swing in order to achieve the "perfect" swing. Art would find him in various contorted positions looking more like a pretzel than a golfer!

67

Walter Davidson, in the saddle, and William S. Harley, seated in the sidecar, on a visit to the Heinz dealership in 1923. Standing, from the left, are Gus Heinz, Art Herrington, and Bert Heinz ready to introduce the "Greatest Motorcycle Ever Built." (But we always knew that!)

MUSHROOM-CHEESE LASAGNA

This fabulous recipe is another that comes by way of the Milwaukee Repertory Theater. Former President of the Friends, Katie Rynkiewicz's enthusiasm and support was always inspiring. This is one of Katie's recipes that is absolutely delicious and is perfect for vegetarians!

Sauce
¼ cup chopped onion
1 clove garlic, minced
2 tablespoons olive oil
2 15-ounce cans tomato purée
¼ cup red wine
1 teaspoon crushed oregano
1 teaspoon salt
½ teaspoon sugar
⅛ teaspoon pepper

Filling
1 pound mushrooms, sliced
4 tablespoons butter or olive oil
½ teaspoon salt
⅛ teaspoon pepper
1 egg, beaten
1 15-ounce package ricotta cheese

6 to 9 lasagna noodles, cooked
4 cups (16 ounces) shredded mozzarella cheese
½ cup Parmesan cheese grated

To make the sauce, in a large saucepan, sauté the onion and garlic in the oil for 5 minutes, or until tender. Add the remaining ingredients. Simmer, uncovered, for 30 minutes. Cool slightly.

To make the filling, sauté the mushrooms in the butter or olive oil for 5 to 10 minutes, or until the liquid has evaporated. Sprinkle with salt and pepper. Set aside. Combine the egg and ricotta. Blend well. Set aside.

To make the lasagne, preheat the oven to 350°F. Spoon just enough sauce to cover the bottom of a 9 by 13-inch baking pan. Begin to layer the noodles, ricotta, mozzarella, and mushrooms. Spoon the sauce over the first layer. Repeat, ending with the sauce. Sprinkle with Parmesan cheese. Bake for about 50 minutes, or until the top is nicely browned. Let stand for 15 minutes before serving. Serves 8.

BREAD STRATA
WITH MUSHROOMS & CHEESE

5 *cloves garlic, minced*
3 *tablespoons olive oil*
1 *28-ounce can crushed tomatoes*
1 *pound mushrooms, sliced thinly*
2 *bunches spinach, washed and*
stemmed
4 *eggs, well beaten*
2 *cups milk*

⅛ *teaspoon nutmeg*
Pinch of salt
Pinch of black pepper
10 *slices French bread, chunked*
2 *tablespoons chopped fresh*
rosemary
½ *cup grated Fontina cheese*
¾ *cup crumbled Gorgonzola cheese*

Lightly oil a 9 by 12-inch baking dish. In a saucepan, heat half of the minced garlic in 1 tablespoon of the olive oil. Add the tomatoes. Cook for 20 minutes over low heat, stirring occasionally. Transfer to a large mixing bowl.

In the same saucepan, add the remaining 2 tablespoons olive oil and the mushrooms. Sauté until limp. Transfer to a bowl. In the saucepan, cook the spinach until wilted. Cool, chop, and add to the mushroom mixture. Season with the remaining garlic. Combine the beaten eggs, milk, and nutmeg and set aside. Season with salt and pepper.

Preheat the oven to 375°F. Spread ¾ cup of the tomato mixture in the oiled baking dish. Add a layer of bread mixture on top, then a layer of mushroom-spinach mixture, and then half of the rosemary and half of the Fontina cheese. Repeat until all of the mixtures are used up. Top with the Gorgonzola cheese. Pour the egg-milk mixture over all. Bake for about 1 hour, or until browned. Cool for 5 minutes. Serve.

A very proud William S. Harley with a copy of the Dodge City Daily Globe announcing another win for Harley-Davidson. The article goes on to say that "Maldwyn Jones on a Harley cut nearly twenty minutes off the world record for 200 miles." It doesn't get much better!

COMFORT CASSEROLE

This casserole is easy and fast. We hope your children like it as much as Carol's boys do!

1 *pound ground beef or turkey (the less fat the better)*
½ *cup finely diced onion*
1 *16-ounce can chopped tomatoes*
Salt and pepper to taste

½ cup shell macaroni (or any shape you have in the cupboard), cooked, or 1 cup cooked Wisconsin wild rice
Shredded cheese (any type you prefer)

Cook the meat until all of the red color is gone. Drain the fat. Sauté the onion and then add the tomatoes. Add salt and pepper to taste. Add the cooked macaroni, or put the cooked wild rice on each plate in the form of a ring and serve the meat in the center. Sprinkle shredded cheese on top.

Carol's two sons—John, left, and Jeffrey, right—having some fun roasting marshmallows at Terry Andrea Park, north of Milwaukee, in 1972. John is a Milwaukee attorney, and Jeff pilots for American Airlines.

CHEESY BREAKFAST SAUSAGE CASSEROLE

This is a modified version of a one-hundred-year-old recipe from Easton, Pennsylvania, home of Margo's great-grandmother, Mary Smith Harley. The stuffing mix is a substitute for cornmeal and various spices. The original recipe did not include cheese, but since Margo was raised in Wisconsin, this recipe does!

1 *pound sausage (your favorite)*
¼ *cup chopped onion*
5 *cups herb-seasoned stuffing mix*
½ *cup chicken broth*
2 *tablespoons butter*

6 *ounces shredded cheddar cheese (extra sharp for a stronger taste)*
2 *cups milk*
⅛ *teaspoon ground black pepper*
5 *eggs, beaten, or 8 ounces egg substitute*

Remove the casings from the sausage. In a large nonstick cooking pan, sauté the sausage and onion until browned. While browning, separate the sausage into small, bite-sized pieces. Drain off any fat. Transfer the cooked sausage and onion into a large mixing bowl. Add the stuffing mix and toss.

Preheat the oven to 350°F. Coat a 9 by 13-inch baking dish with oil or cooking spray. Transfer the sausage mixture to the baking pan and form one even layer. In the mixing bowl, gently pour the chicken broth and melted butter over the sausage and stuffing mixture. Toss, sprinkle the shredded cheese, and toss again. Combine the milk, pepper, and eggs in a bowl. Whisk together thoroughly. Pour the milk mixture over the sausage mixture in the baking pan. Bake for 40 to 45 minutes, or until completely set. Before serving, let the casserole rest for 5 minutes. Serves 8.

BEST-EVER ZUCCHINI-SQUASH PIE

This can be the "main event" when served with a tossed salad, or use it as a side dish—a great way to use up summer squash. And it is an excellent meal for vegetarians!

1 *8-ounce can prepared crescent rolls*
2 *teaspoons Dijon-style mustard*
¼ *cup butter or margarine*
1½ *pounds zucchini, sliced thin*
1 *medium onion, chopped*
1 *clove garlic, minced*
¼ *cup chopped fresh parsley*

½ *teaspoon dried basil*
½ *teaspoon dried oregano*
½ *teaspoon dried thyme*
½ *teaspoon salt*
2 *large eggs*
¼ *cup milk*
8 *ounces mozzarella cheese, shredded*

Preheat the oven to 350°F. Remove the crescent rolls from the container, unroll, and press the dough along the bottom and sides of an ungreased 10-inch pie pan. Bake for about 5 to 6 minutes, or until lightly browned. Cool. Spread the mustard over the crust.

In a large skillet, melt the butter. Add the onion and garlic. Sauté and gently stir. Add the zucchini and continue to sauté for about 5 to 6 minutes, or until the zucchini is tender but not limp. Combine the parsley, basil, oregano, thyme, salt, and pepper. Add the spice mixture to the zucchini, remove from the heat, and set aside.

In a large bowl, whisk the eggs and milk together. Blend well. Add the zucchini mixture and combine well. Add the cheese and blend. Pour into the pie plate with the crescent roll crust. Bake at 350°F for 25 minutes, or until a knife inserted in the center comes out clean.

The children of the Harley and Davidson founders always played together during their childhood. If they were not swimming at Pine Lake, they were over at the Harley's, on Beaver Lake. From the left: Allan Davidson, Gordon Davidson, Ann Harley (Margo's mom), Bobbie Davidson, Margaret Davidson, Ann Davidson, Arthur Davidson, Jr., Marion Davidson (Carol's mom), and John Harley.

"The Celebrated Harley"

YOU CAN'T HEAR THE
"SILENT GRAY FELLOW"

K
VP Co

THE K.V.P. ROOSTER
DIVIDES HIS FEED
WITH THE
SILENT GRAY FELLOW
DEC. 21, 1912,
MILWAUKEE ATHLETIC
CLUB
10:30 P. M. TO "5-35" H. D.

Chicken Feed

K. V. P. ROOSTER-TAIL.

RED ENAMELED MECHANICAL BI-VALVES.

GASOLINE.
Clutch in Neutral.

"RED HEAD" SPARK PLUGS.
ANNULAR BALL BEARINGS.
HEXAGON NUTS, SALTED.   BATTERY CELL-ERY.

MORE GASOLINE.
Shift to First Speed.

VACUUM FED TENDERLOIN, with Ful-Floteing
Bearings.
HEAT TREATED ROLLER BEARINGS.
INFLATED ROLLS.

STILL MORE GASOLINE.
Shift to Second Speed.

TROXEL SALAD, with H-D Oil Dressing.

STILL MUCH MORE GASOLINE.
Wide Open.

CONDENSED ODORS, with Raybeston Discs.

INDIAN FIREWATER.
Shift to Reverse.

H. D. Magneto Floro-Fizz.
NIERSTEINER Picric Acid—Ether—Gasoline Special

Discords by The H. D. Trio.
Soloist,   Pordy Whistle.
Piano, O. Pen Exhaust.
Cello, Q. T. Muffler.

The evening of December 21, 1912, "The Celebrated Harley," as the invitation states, was honored by his friends at the Milwaukee Athletic Club for his valued inventions contributing to the design and continued development of the Harley-Davidson motorcycle. The menu consisted of Hexagon Nuts, Gasoline (cocktails), Vacuum-Fed Tenderloin with Ful-Floteing Bearings, Inflated Rolls, and Troxel Salad with H-D Oil Dressing. Sounds like delicious fun!

Harleys and Davidsons Celebrate

Indeed, all four founders had much to celebrate! And they did so often. Many family dinners took place at the Milwaukee Athletic Club. The families gathered together during holidays and other special occasions.

During their leisure hours, members of the Harley and Davidson families enjoyed fishing, hunting wild game, and camping out. The bounty they caught was brought to one of the mothers or sisters to cook and serve to the happy hunters and the rest of the families.

William Harley was not only an avid sportsman, he was an accomplished artist and keen observer of nature and wildlife. Art Davidson, Jr., recalled (and legend has it) that Bill Harley mounted a camera on a rifle expressly to take photos in the wild. In the privacy of his art studio, he produced studies and sketches, and from those studies, engravings. Pen-and-ink drawings were made, which he gave as gifts to his closest friends and his family. This section includes one of those engravings.

Directly following his win at the Federation of American Motorcyclists August 1910 Endurance Run, this picture was taken and printed in the November 1910 issue of Motorcycling. *In that issue, it states that William Harley was the last founder to marry.*

ASIAN CURRIED CABBAGE

1 *tablespoon olive oil*
½ *cup diced onions*
2 *cloves garlic, minced*
1½ *tablespoons whole-grain Dijon-style mustard*
2 *teaspoon curry powder*
1 *teaspoon ground turmeric*
3 *pounds green cabbage, thinly sliced (12 cups)*

¼ *cup fat-free, low-sodium chicken broth*
¼ *cup rice wine vinegar*
½ *teaspoon salt*
¼ *teaspoon black pepper*
1 *tablespoon sesame seeds, lightly toasted*

Sauté the onions and garlic in a large frying pan until golden brown. Add the mustard, curry, and turmeric and stir frequently. Add the cabbage, broth, vinegar, salt, and pepper. Toss frequently until al dente (soft enough to be cooked through but still firm). Top with sesame seeds. Serves 6 to 8.

FAR EAST CELERY

2 *cups sliced celery*
1 *8-ounce can sliced water chestnuts*
1 *can cream of mushroom soup*

Buttered bread crumbs
Salt to taste
Grated Parmesan cheese (optional)

Preheat the oven to 350°F. Cook the celery in 2 cups salted water until just tender. Drain. Add the water chestnuts and undiluted mushroom soup. Mix well. Pour into a well-greased casserole. Top with buttered bread crumbs and season with salt to taste. Bake for 30 minutes. Sprinkle grated Parmesan cheese on top. Serves 6.

YUMMY GREEN BEANS

2 *pounds fresh greens beans, ends*
trimmed
2 *tablespoons butter*
2 *tablespoons walnut oil*
Lemon juice

Salt and pepper to taste
1 *cup chopped walnuts (about*
3¾ ounces), toasted
2 *tablespoons minced fresh parsley*

Cook the beans in a large pot of boiling lightly salted water for about 5 minutes, or until just tender. Drain and rinse immediately in cold water. Drain well, place in a bowl, and set aside. Add the butter and walnut oil in a large heavy skillet over high heat. Drizzle just a little bit of lemon juice over the beans and toss. Add to the skillet and cook for about 4 minutes, or until heated through. Season with salt and pepper to taste. Add the chopped walnuts and parsley and toss. Serve in your favorite bowl. Serves 8.

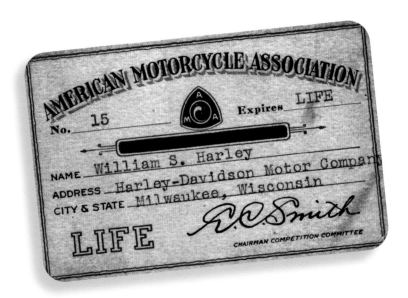

Eventually, the Federation of American Motorcyclists became the American Motorcycle Association. Immediately following the formation of the new organization, William S. Harley received his life membership, number 15, in Daytona, Florida.

CARROTS IN HORSERADISH

A very simple but delicious recipe for the holidays. Carol invented this dish for Thanksgiving.

2 *bunches carrots, peeled and sliced lengthwise*
2 *tablespoons prepared horseradish*
1 *cup mayonnaise*
2 *tablespoons water*

1 *tablespoon grated onion*
¼ *cup seasoned bread crumbs*
Butter
Salt and pepper to taste

Preheat the oven to 350°F. Parboil the carrots until almost tender. Place in an 8 by 11-inch casserole dish. Mix the horseradish, mayonnaise, water, and onion with the carrots. Brown the bread crumbs in butter, stirring often and being very careful not to burn. Spread the bread crumbs over the carrots. Bake for 15 to 20 minutes. This dish can be made and baked the day before, and then reheated before serving. Serves 6.

AND EVEN MORE CARROTS

These carrots are slooooow cooked, easy to prepare, and great for every day or for special occasions. Caraway adds an interesting flavor.

3 *pounds carrots*
4 *tablespoons butter*
½ *teaspoon salt*

1 *teaspoon sugar*
1 *cup water*
½ *teaspoon caraway seeds*

Peel the carrots, cut in half lengthwise, then cut into 1-inch pieces. In a large frying pan, combine the carrots, butter, salt, sugar, and water. Simmer, stirring occasionally, for about 1 hour, or until the water evaporates. Add the caraway seeds and continue cooking for about 15 minutes, or until the carrots are tender and start to turn golden brown. Watch carefully so that they don't burn! Serves 8.

COOKED CUCUMBERS
À LA JEFFREY DAVIDSON SCHRAGER

When Jeff and John were children, Carol always made this simple dish for them. Carol usually made it with zucchini. One night, not having any zucchini, she substituted cucumbers. The best recipes are developed from adapting existing recipes. Almost any recipe we share with you can be modified and changed to suit your tastes. So many times, necessity is the mother of invention!

Pickle or Japanese cucumbers　　*Salt and pepper to taste*
Butter　　*Sliced green onions*
Lemon juice to taste

Peel and seed the cucumbers and slice lengthwise into long strips. Gently sauté the cucumbers in some butter. Add lemon juice, salt, and pepper to taste. Sprinkle with sliced green onions.

*Carol and her two sons, Jeffrey and John, celebrating Christmas Eve dinner.
On the far left is Mark Antonides, a family friend.*

William S. Harley is the driver, plowing through the snow on Highland Boulevard in Milwaukee.

MAGGIE KOHLER'S CHICKEN

2 *boned chicken breasts*
1 *16-ounce can chicken broth*
1 *bunch fresh asparagus spears*
1½ *to* **2** *cans cream of chicken soup*
1 *cup mayonnaise*

½ teaspoon curry powder
2 *teaspoons fresh lemon juice*
1 *cup sliced mushrooms (optional)*
Bread crumbs
Paprika

Preheat the oven to 325°F. Simmer the chicken breasts in the chicken broth for 25 minutes, or until partially cooked. Cook the asparagus until al dente. Drain well. Combine the cream of chicken soup, mayonnaise, curry powder, and lemon juice. Place the asparagus in a flat buttered casserole and cover with the chicken, mushrooms, and sauce. Top with bread crumbs and dust with paprika for color. Bake for 35 to 45 minutes, or until bubbly. Serves 4.

GILROY FORTY-CLOVE GARLIC CHICKEN

Every year, the city of Gilroy, California, which is very near to Hollister, plays host to the famous Garlic Festival. Gilroy is a favorite spot for great shopping, arts and crafts, and of course, wonderful food.

6 *to* **8** *chicken pieces (any parts you wish)*
40 *cloves fresh garlic, peeled*
½ cup dry white wine
¼ cup dry vermouth
¼ cup olive oil
4 *ribs celery, thickly sliced*

2 *tablespoons finely chopped fresh parsley*
2 *teaspoons dried basil*
1 *teaspoon dried oregano*
Pinch of crushed red pepper
Juice of 1 lemon
Salt and pepper to taste

Preheat the oven to 350°F. Place the chicken in a baking dish. Combine the garlic, wine, vermouth, oil, celery, parsley, basil, oregano, and red pepper. Pour over the chicken. Squeeze the lemon juice over the chicken and add salt and pepper to taste. Cover with aluminum foil and bake for 40 minutes. Uncover and bake for another 15 minutes. Serves 4 to 6.

DAVIDSON FAMILY BEEF STEW

This is a very simple and delicious stew for cold Wisconsin winters.

2 *pounds beef stew meat*
Oil
1 *package dry onion soup mix*

1 *can cream of mushroom soup*
1 *cup Burgundy wine*
Potatoes (optional)

Preheat the oven to 325°F. In a large frying skillet, brown the meat and set aside. In a large mixing bowl, combine the onion soup mix, mushroom soup, and wine and blend well. Add the meat and stir. Transfer to a baking dish and cover. Bake for 1½ hours. If you wish, add some potatoes after 30 minutes of the cooking time.

HARLEY FAMILY PERFECTION MEATLOAF

Margo fondly remembers her mom making meatloaf. Her mom, Ann Harley, always served meatloaf with baked potatoes. The next day, if any meatloaf was left over, the family would slice it up and make sandwiches. This recipe is true comfort food.

2 *to* **3** *pounds ground hamburger, pork, or veal*
1 *egg*
½ cup chopped onion
¾ cup seasoned bread crumbs or day-old bread, torn into small pieces

½ cup catsup
2 *tablespoons Worcestershire sauce or soy sauce*
Salt and black pepper to taste
Sliced dill pickle
1 *cup grated cheddar cheese*
Baked potatoes (optional)

Preheat the oven to 350°F. In a large mixing bowl, combine the meat, egg, onion, bread crumbs, catsup, Worcestershire, and salt and pepper to taste. Knead and blend thoroughly just until mixed. Roll the meat mixture out onto the counter top and form into a loaf. Place in a loaf pan and bake for 45 to 60 minutes or longer, until the meat is thoroughly cooked. About 10 minutes before the meatloaf is finished, cover the top with catsup, sliced pickles, and shredded cheese. Serves 4 to 6.

William S. Harley was not only a gifted engineer and designer, he was a keen observer of nature and a talented artist. In his precious free time, Bill Harley sketched, primarily scenes of wildlife, and then went into his studio and made engravings of selected sketches. This is one of his rare engravings depicting his hunting lodge, "Camp Lookout," in South Dakota. Bill Harley gave these engravings to only his closest friends and family, usually for Christmas or birthday presents.

87

WILD DUCKS

This recipe comes to us from Helen Davidson and Ellen Whyte's *Choice Family Recipes.* Since all of our grandfathers and fathers enjoyed fishing and hunting, our grandmothers and mothers became skilled cooks, preparing all sorts of wild game—anything from grouse and venison to ducks.

Instead of using this dressing, you may want to fill the duck cavities with with celery stalk; cored, peeled, and sliced apple; and quartered onion.

Dressing
¼ cup chopped onion
¼ cup butter, melted
4 cups cubed day-old bread
¼ cup chopped parsley
½ cup chopped celery
½ teaspoon salt
½ teaspoon paprika

⅛ teaspoon nutmeg
2 eggs
½ cup milk

5 ducks, fully plucked including
   pin feathers
2½ teaspoons salt
5 teaspoons butter, softened

To make the dressing, sauté the onion in melted butter. In a large bowl, combine the bread, parsley, celery, salt, paprika, and nutmeg. Blend and toss well. Add the sautéed onion and blend well. In a small mixing bowl, whisk the milk and eggs together. Combine the bread and egg mixtures until lightly moistened.

To roast the ducks, preheat the oven to 400°F. Clean and wash the ducks thoroughly in cold water. Dry inside and out. Rub the inside with ½ teaspoon salt and 1 teaspoon butter per duck. Mix the dressing ingredients together. Fill the cavities of ducks with dressing. Securely fasten with toothpicks and string. Place on a rack in a shallow roasting pan, uncovered. Decrease the heat to 250°F and bake for 3 to 4 hours depending on the size of the ducks. Occasionally pierce the skin to drain the fat. *Hints:* For lean ducks, place 1 to 2 strips of bacon over the top of each duck. If the ducks start browning early in the cooking cycle, lightly cover with aluminum foil.

When ready to serve, pop back in a 500°F oven to quickly brown and crisp the skin. Garnish the ducks with orange slices and serve with currant or cranberry jelly.

*Celebrating Grandmother Davidson's eightieth birthday at the Milwaukee
Athletic Club. Starting with the little boy in front and moving clockwise:
Jimmy Davidson; his father, Arthur Davidson, Sr.; Mary Davidson; Helen
Davidson Morton and her husband, Godfrey Morton; Margaret Davidson
Nelson; William Davidson; Allan Davidson; Gordon Davidson; Carol's mom,
Marion "Midge" Davidson; Henry Marx, Sr.; Maimie Davidson; "Tiger" Marx;
Emma Davidson; next two individuals are unidentified; Bobby Davidson; Elsie
Johnson; Walter Davidson, Sr.; John Marx; Arthur Davidson, Jr.; Clara Davidson;
William Davidson, Sr.; Ruth Davidson Winding; and Grandmother Davidson,
mother of the three Davidson founders.*

HARLEY FAMILY BAKED PHEASANT

Margo's grandfather, father, and brothers all enjoyed hunting and bringing home wild game birds (pheasant, grouse, partridge, duck, and squab guinea hen). We would be remiss not mentioning Erwin Eichstaedt. Erwin was the proprietor of Erwin's Meat Market, just off 49th and Lloyd Streets in Milwaukee. For decades, the Harley and Davidson families would bring their fowl to Erwin. He would completely dress out the game birds for our Sunday dinners. Erwin was a master butcher, and when he retired, Milwaukee lost one of its best corner markets.

When a cut of meat is very lean, the butcher takes a large, hollow needle filled with thin strips of fat (called lardons) and threads it under the skin or into the muscle. The meat is then rendered moist and tender. A pheasant may need to be larded or wrapped with a piece of fatty ham, bacon, or prosciutto.

Orange Sauce
2 *large oranges*
1 *cup orange juice*
¼ *cup orange-flavored liquor*
3 *tablespoons sugar*
2 *tablespoons Dijon-style mustard*
2 *tablespoons butter or margarine*

1 *tablespoon red currant jelly*
1 *tablespoon brandy*

2 *pheasants (2 to 2½ pounds each)*
Salt
1 *orange, washed and halved*
2 *sprigs fresh thyme*

To make the orange sauce, remove the outer peel from the oranges and slice into thin strips. Juice the peeled oranges. Place the peel in a medium saucepan and cover with water. Bring the mixture to a boil over high heat. Drain the peel and add ½ cup of the orange juice, the orange flavored liquor, and sugar to the pan. Boil over high heat, uncovered, until the liquid is almost gone. Do not scorch. Remove 2 tablespoons of the peel and set aside. To the pan, add the remaining ½ cup orange juice, Dijon mustard, red currant jelly, and brandy. Stir over medium heat until blended well and the jelly melts. Set aside.

To prepare the pheasants, preheat the oven to 400°F. Thoroughly rinse the birds with cold water inside and out. Dry completely. Rub salt inside of the cavities. Place half an orange and 1 sprig of thyme in the body cavity of each bird. Truss the skin, closing the body cavity. Cover the bottom of the pan with ½ inch water. Place the pheasants breast down in the roasting pan.

Roast the pheasants for 15 minutes. Turn the birds over and brush with the orange sauce. Decrease the heat to 325°F and roast for another 50 minutes, or until the juices run slightly pink when the skin is pierced. Baste often while roasting. Let stand for at least 10 minutes before serving.

To serve, skim the fat from the pheasant drippings. Add the drippings to the orange sauce. Boil over high heat, uncovered, until reduced to 1 cup. Garnish the pheasants with the orange peel set aside from sauce and serve with the orange sauce. Serves 6 to 8.

A good day's hunt! Margo's dad, Charles Kohl, and her brother Charles after a successful day of hunting pheasants. Her dad would bring the pheasant home and immediately bring them to Erwin, the corner master butcher on Lloyd Street. Erwin would dress the pheasant out, ready to be cooked.

  Margo shows off her Harley-Davidson 100th Anniversary jacket.

BRINE-CURED ROAST TURKEY

Margo came upon this recipe and adapted it. It is the best turkey—very moist and tender because it is cured in brine. This recipe uses a lot of spices, but you will find, it's well worth it. It is the only way to cook a turkey! After brining, the turkey can be stuffed with your favorite stuffing. Turkeys cook faster when not stuffed. If you are in a hurry, stuffing can be made on the stove top with some of the savory juices from cooking. Margo served this for Carol at Thanksgiving 2002. Now Carol is a believer!

Brine
1¼ *cups kosher salt*
3¼ *cups sugar*
2 *cups honey*
4 *to* **6** *sprigs each fresh parsley, dill, thyme, and sage*
2 *sprigs fresh rosemary*
2 *tablespoons fennel seeds*
2 *tablespoons black peppercorns*
2 *whole cinnamon sticks*
5 *bay leaves*

8 *cloves*
1 *tablespoon juniper berries*
1 *tablespoon allspice*
2 *lemons, cut in half and seeded*
2 *gallons boiling water (it is best to use bottled water)*

1 *16- to 18-pound turkey*
Butter
Fresh rosemary

To prepare the brine, combine all of the ingredients in a large container, pouring the boiling water in last. Stir well to blend and cool to room temperature. Add the turkey, cover, and refrigerate overnight.

To roast the turkey, the next day, remove the turkey from the brine and rinse off under cold water.

Preheat the oven to 300°F. Cover the turkey with cheesecloth and place in a large roasting pan. Saturate the cheesecloth with butter. Roast for 3 to 4 hours, basting every half hour, until the thigh temperature reaches 150°F on a meat thermometer. For the last 15 minutes of cooking, gently remove the cheesecloth in order to brown the turkey.

Remove the turkey from the oven and let rest for 30 minutes. Transfer the turkey to a serving platter. Garnish with fresh rosemary. Serves 8 to 10.

LEONA'S ORANGE CHICKEN

Leona is Carol's friend from Carmel, California.

1 *quartered chicken*
Dixie Fry or any chicken bread
  crumb mixture
Butter
Garlic powder

Salt and pepper
Grated fresh ginger
1 *can frozen orange juice, defrosted*
Sliced water chestnuts

Preheat the oven to 325°F. Coat the chicken with Dixie Fry or bread crumb mixture. Brown in some butter. Place in a casserole with the skin down. Sprinkle garlic powder, salt, pepper, and ginger over all. Cover with undiluted orange juice and sliced water chestnuts. Cook for 45 to 60 minutes, or until the chicken is tender.

BAKED SESAME CHICKEN

3 *tablespoons melted butter*
¼ *cup soy sauce*
1 *clove fresh garlic, minced*

3 *tablespoons sesame seeds*
1 *2½- to 3-pound fryer, cut up*

Preheat the oven to 350°F. Combine the melted butter, soy sauce, and garlic in a 2-quart casserole. Spread the sesame seeds on waxed paper. Roll the chicken parts in the butter mixture, then in the sesame seeds, and place in the casserole. Bake for 40 to 45 minutes, or until the chicken is golden brown. Serve hot or cold with rice and fruit or tossed salad. Serves 4.

Margo's uncle John and aunt Kay Harley are in this classic photo taken in Daytona. Uncle John was Manager of Industrial Affairs for the company but began as a draftsman in the engineering department. Always actively involved in advancing the sport of motorcycling, John E. Harley was awarded the American Motorcycling Association's highest tribute, the Dud Perkins Award. The purpose of the award is to acknowledge the highest level of service to the A.M.A., and the recipients are individuals whose contributions are nationally recognized. William S. Harley was also a recipient of this award.

Like father like son! John E. Harley, Jr., and his wife, Kate, also enjoy riding when they are not tending to their farm and donkeys. John and Kate both love raising donkeys and have amassed quite a menagerie of ceramic donkeys. Just like his father and grandfather before him, John is an avid outdoorsman. And just like his father who served during World War II, John served his country in Vietnam.

RAGOUT OF LAMB

This scrumptious recipe comes from Maja Jurisic, one of the best cooks Margo knows. Maja and her husband, Don Fraker, have been cooking Sundown Suppers for many years. Sundown Suppers are a tradition at the Milwaukee Repertory Theater. Every Saturday during the run of a show, actors, staff, technicians, and stagehands are served a hot home-cooked meal in between the two shows. This ragout is one of Maja's specialties. The length of time that it takes to cook allows all the flavors to blend in a gastronomic delight. Enjoy!

2 *pounds boneless lamb (ask butcher to trim well), cut into 1-inch cubes*
Salt and pepper to taste
6 *tablespoons olive oil*
4 *onions chopped (Vidalia are best)*
2 *large cloves garlic, minced*

1 *tablespoon flour*
1 *cup hearty red wine (such as Cabernet Sauvignon or Burgundy)*
3 *cups beef broth*
⅜ *cup tomato paste*
2 *bay leaves*

In a large mixing bowl, sprinkle the meat with salt and pepper. Marinate for 10 minutes. Heat 2 tablespoons of the olive oil over high heat. Quickly brown the lamb to evenly sear in the juices, adding more oil if necessary. After lamb is browned, drain in a colander over a bowl to reserve the juices. In a large pan, sauté the onions in 2 tablespoons of the olive oil and add the garlic. Add the flour and wine to form a roux. Stir until thickened. Add the beef broth and tomato paste and stir constantly until thick. Remove from the heat.

Preheat the oven to 350°F. In a Dutch oven or ovenproof casserole, combine all of the ingredients, including juices, and mix well. Cook for 2 to 3 hours. Serve with rice, noodles, or mashed potatoes—you be the chef!

Ann Mary Harley, daughter of William S. Harley, in a high school photo from the 1920s.

ANN HARLEY'S FAMILY LAMB SHANKS

Margo's mom cooked lamb all the time. Her children did not share her enthusiasm for lamb, so she kept experimenting to develop a recipe that her children would find edible! She won them over when she braised the lamb shanks, added condensed onion soup, and baked the dish until the meat fell off the bone. Margo took her basic recipe and embellished it again and again. She named this recipe in honor of her mom. It fills the entire house with such pleasant aromas! Serve with rice or buttered boiled potatoes and a tossed salad.

4 lamb shanks (ask butcher to crack them)
1 tablespoon oil
1 large onion, diced
1 clove garlic, minced
1 large celery stalk, peeled and diced
3 medium carrots, peeled and diced
2 tablespoons grated fresh ginger
1 cup red wine
3 cups low-sodium chicken broth

4 plum tomatoes, seeded and diced
1 tablespoon grated lemon rind
¼ teaspoon ground cumin
¼ teaspoon ground coriander
¼ teaspoon ground cinnamon
½ teaspoon crushed red pepper flakes
1 large bay leaf
Salt and pepper to taste
Parsley
½ cup minced fresh cilantro leaves

In a large heavy-duty saucepan, braise the lamb shanks until browned all over. Remove and set aside. To the same pan, add the oil, onion, garlic, celery, carrots, and ginger. Sauté, stirring frequently, for about 5 minutes. Remove and set aside. Add the wine, broth, tomatoes, lemon rind, cumin, coriander, cinnamon, red pepper flakes, and bay leaf. Return the lamb shanks and vegetable mixture to the pan. Partially cover and simmer slowly for about 2½ to 3 hours, or until the meat begins to fall off the bone. When cooking is completed, discard the bay leaf. Season with salt and pepper to taste. To serve, place a lamb shank on a plate and ladle sauce over it. Garnish with parsley and cilantro. Serves 4.

SCHWEINBRATEN À LA JACHTHUBER

Bavarian Roast Pork

When in Germany discovering Grandmother Harley's roots, Margo stayed with her cousins Hans and Brigitte Jachthuber. They served such wonderful meals. The food just kept coming out of the kitchen. And the Bavarian wine was so wonderful. Bavarians are some of the most hospitable people in the world! This is a delicious dish from Hans and Brigitte. The dish is great to serve with cooked red cabbage.

2½ *pounds pork loin*
1 *large onion, chopped*
2 *stalks celery, chopped*

2 *leeks, cleaned and chopped*
2 *cups water*
¼ *cup dry white wine*

Preheat the oven to 400°F. In a large frying pan, braise and sear the meat on all sides in its own fat and juices. Add the onion, celery, leeks, and water. Cover the pan and roast for 2½ hours. After 1 hour, decrease the heat to 350°F and turn the roast. When tender, remove the roast and strain the juices from the cooking pan. Serve au jus or make a gravy by combining the juices and wine with a small amount of cornstarch and cold water. Serves 4.

BAVARIAN SPÄTZLE

Bavarian Pasta

4 *cups flour, sifted*
3 *eggs, lightly beaten*
½ *cup milk*

½ *teaspoon salt*
Butter
Sour cream

In a bowl, combine the flour, eggs, milk, and salt to form a very soft dough. Knead the dough until it forms soft blisters. In a saucepan, bring some salted water to a boil. Decrease the heat and maintain a simmer. Place a colander over the pan and pour about ¼ of the batter into the colander. Press the dough through the holes with a wooden spoon or spatula into the hot water. The spätzle will start to swell and float to the surface of the water. Remove from the water and drain. Place in a serving bowl with a dollop of butter and sour cream.

Carol's black cocker, Molly, is just waiting for that Christmas roast beef to fall on the floor!

In Seattle, Carol visited Pike's Market and received an unexpected hug from the manager of the fish department.

FRAGRANT SALMON WITH GREEN SAUCE

Maja Jurisic, a physician, recognizes the health benefits to be gained from all of the "good" omega-3 fatty acids found in salmon. However, she is not happy with the fishy odor that lingers when making salmon. One evening, Maja experimented, adapting something she saw on a PBS show called *New Nordic Cooking.* When Don (her tall, blue-eyed, possibly Nordic, and definitely charming husband) came down for dinner, he said, "What is that great smell? The air is fragrant." And he was right. Poaching salmon like this perfumes the kitchen with a light lemony scent. This recipe can easily be expanded or contracted as needed—just be careful not to skimp on the lemon slices.

The green sauce was the result of the happy serendipity that sometimes occurs when you just throw together what you happen to have lying around. Earlier in the day, Maja sprained her foot and used a bag of frozen peas to get the swelling down. Taking the defrosted peas, Maja added some other ingredients she found in the fridge and came up with a sauce to accompany the fragrant salmon.

Green Sauce
*½ bag of frozen peas, thawed and
   cooked*
1 *bunch fresh basil*
⅛ cup buttermilk
Juice of half a lemon
Salt and pepper to taste

1 *bunch parsley*
2 *to* **4** *salmon fillets*
1 *lemon, thinly sliced*

To make the green sauce, blend the peas, basil, buttermilk, lemon, and salt and pepper in a blender.

To make the salmon, layer half of the bunch of parsley in a poacher. Place the salmon fillets skin-side down on top of the parsley. Layer the lemon slices on top of the salmon fillets. Place the rest of the parsley on top of the lemons. Fill with water to cover the salmon and cook until the salmon is done. (Maja prefers well-cooked fish. She brings it to a boil and then simmers it for about 10 minutes). Remove the skin. Serve the salmon with the green sauce.

MARGO'S FAVORITE SALMON

This recipe is so incredibly easy—and just as scrumptious! Margo's dad liked to fish and her mom would always flour-coat and pan fry what he caught. One night, having only the following ingredients, Margo concocted this recipe. Hope that you enjoy it, too!

*Any amount of salmon fillets that
  you want to cook*

*Pico de gallo (see recipe below)
Sour cream*

Broil the salmon fillets in the oven or, better yet, on the grill. Serving salmon that is slightly rare makes the cooking time only a few minutes on each side. After the salmon fillets are finished broiling, top with a generous portion of pico de gallo and then with a dollop of sour cream. Serve immediately.

PICO DE GALLO

Pico de gallo literally means "rooster's beak" and refers to the way roosters eat by chopping their food into rough pieces. It is best to prepare this salsa a day ahead to allow all the flavors to blend together. Add the heat—whatever level you prefer—at the end of the recipe. More heat can be added, but it is next to impossible to take any away. Margo prefers jalapeño or serrano peppers. If you want to add extra flavor, grill all the vegetables first. Yum!

8 *plum tomatoes, seeded and
  chopped coarsely*
1 *medium onion, diced fine*
3 *cloves garlic, minced*
1 *bunch or more fresh cilantro
  leaves and stems, chopped*

1 *cup fresh lime juice*
Salt
*Jalapeño, serrano, crushed red
  pepper flakes, or ground cayenne
  pepper to taste (optional)*

Carefully wash all of the ingredients. Combine the tomatoes, onion, garlic, cilantro, and lime juice and mix well. If the sauce is too thick, thin it out with water or tomato juice. Add salt to taste. You can add your heat at this point. Spice it to your tastes. Carefully cut up, seed, and pith the peppers. Mince very fine and add to the mixture. Makes about 2 cups.

Allan Davidson with his prized catch of the day! Allan was the son of William A. Davidson and an uncle to Carol. He always used to tease Carol when she was a youngster.

you and the kids.
It is queer just as soon
as I get away on a trip
like this I suddenly
find out how much
I love you. I hope
you are all well and
be prepared to welcome
your hubby when he
returns
                with love
                    Shel

Mrs Wm S Harley
4906 Washington Blvd
Milwaukee Wis.
    U.S.A.

Everything Sweet for the Sweets

Both the Harleys and Davidsons came from families with what is now called "strong family values." Both families wanted their children to be successful and find their own way in life. If that eventually meant working for the company, it was accepted. A son of one of the founders started at the bottom and worked his way up the career ladder. Not until recently has a daughter worked for the company.

William Davidson was the first to marry in 1903, followed by Arthur in 1908, then Walter in 1910. Later that year, Bill Harley was the last to marry. Between them, fourteen children were born, who, in turn, married and had children of their own. The four founders' children were constant companions. As Art Davidson, Jr., recalls, "I spent more time at the Harley home than my own!" With husbands away during World War II, Ann Harley and many of the Davidson wives formed a club, sometimes playing cards, but many times volunteering at the Curative Workshop. They were a close group.

In his West Side High School (renamed West Division, and now called High School of the Arts) yearbook, William S. Harley was called the "vagabond gentleman." Here he is on graduation day with three of his classmates.

GRANDMA HARLEY'S PEACH COBBLER

Filling
¼ cup white sugar
¼ brown sugar
2 tablespoons flour
½ teaspoon cinnamon
¼ teaspoon nutmeg
2 teaspoons cornstarch
4 to 6 cups fresh peeled peaches
1 teaspoon fresh lemon juice

Cobbler
1 cup flour
¼ cup white sugar
¼ brown sugar
1 teaspoon baking powder
½ teaspoon salt
3 ounces unsalted butter
2 eggs, slightly beaten
¼ cup half-and-half

Topping
Sugar
Cinnamon

Preheat the oven to 425°F. To make the filling, in a large bowl, combine both of the sugars, flour, cinnamon, nutmeg, and cornstarch. Mix well. In a small bowl, combine the peaches and lemon juice. Combine with the flour mixture. Turn out into a 2-quart baking dish. Bake for 10 minutes.

Meanwhile, to make the cobbler, combine the flour, both of the sugars, baking powder, and salt in a large bowl. Blend well. With a pastry cutter (or two knives) cut the butter into small bits until it forms a coarse crumbly mixture. Stir in half-and-half until just combined.

Remove the peaches from the oven. Drop spoonfuls of the filling over all. Sprinkle the entire cobbler with the sugar and cinnamon mixture. Bake for about 30 minutes, or until the topping is golden.

TRADITIONAL DAVIDSON FAMILY BIRTHDAY CAKE

In honor of Helen Davidson Morton's fortieth birthday, Helen and her friend Ellen baked the birthday cake recipe from their cookbook and treated all the children at the Milwaukee Children's Hospital to a slice of this delicious family favorite. The children loved it and from then on Helen and Ellen made certain that if a child was in the hospital on his or her birthday, the child received one of their homemade birthday cakes!

This recipe is an original recipe from Mrs. William C. Davidson, mother of the three Davidson brothers who cofounded the motorcycle company with their friend William S. Harley.

Custard Filling
1 *egg*
3 *tablespoons sugar*
⅛ *teaspoon salt*
2 *tablespoons flour*
1 *cup scalded milk*
1 *tablespoon butter*
1 *teaspoon vanilla*

Batter
1⅓ *cups cake flour*
2 *teaspoons baking powder*

8 *egg yolks*
1 *cup sugar, sifted*
½ *cup boiling water*
½ *teaspoon salt*
1 *teaspoon vanilla*

Milk Chocolate Frosting
¼ *pound butter*
5 *tablespoons sugar*
1 *egg*
1½ *square bitter chocolate, melted*

To make the custard filling, thoroughly the beat the egg. Add the sugar, salt, and flour. Add the hot milk, stirring constantly. Continue stirring until mixture thickens and a coating forms on the spoon. Add the butter. Cool. Add the vanilla.

To make the batter, preheat the oven to 400°F. Sift the flour. Measure and sift three times with the baking powder. Beat the egg yolks in a bowl until light. Gradually add the sifted sugar to the yolk mixture while constantly beating. Add the hot water, salt, and flour mixture to the egg mixture. Add the vanilla and mix. Pour into three greased and floured 9-inch layer cake pans. Bake for 10 to 15 minutes. *Warning:* Be careful sampling the batter; consuming raw or undercooked eggs may increase your risk of food-borne illness.

Meanwhile, to make the frosting, cream the butter and sugar. Add the egg and beat well. Add the chocolate and beat at high speed until the frosting is light in color and creamy.

When the cake is done, invert the pans to cool. Fill the layers with the custard filling and frost with the milk chocolate frosting.

Carol alongside a Harley in California, giving a big thumbs-up for one hundred years of Harley-Davidson!

Harley family portrait. From the left: William James; his mother, Anna Caroline; his father, William Sylvester; Margo's mother, Ann Mary; and John Edward. The boys are pretty cute in those knickers!

HARLEY FAMILY EASY NO-BAKE
CHOCOLATE REFRIGERATOR ROLL

Ann Harley loved this dessert—mainly because there is absolutely no cooking! As a cook, Margo's mom was wonderfully inventive, but when it came to desserts she would go to one of the many German bakeries in Milwaukee. This dessert should be made the same day of your dinner. You can try different types of wafers, such as cappuccino, almond, pumpkin, oatmeal, or chocolate mint. The important thing to remember: the wafers need to be thin. This dessert is best when real whipped cream is used. If you are watching calories and cholesterol, commercial topping in a tub can be substituted. Chocolate Refrigerator Roll is easy to make during the busy winter holidays. Margo suspects her mom first found the recipe on the box of Nabisco chocolate wafers.

2 *cups heavy cream*
1 *teaspoon pure vanilla extract*
3 *tablespoons granulated sugar*

1 *package Nabisco Famous Chocolate Wafers or another type of thin wafer*
Chocolate curls, crushed peppermint candy, etc., for garnish

Beat together the cream, vanilla, and sugar in a medium-sized bowl until stiff peaks form. Spread the whipped cream on each wafer. Stack together and stand on end to begin forming a log. Place some whipped cream on the center of the serving dish and set the first section on end. Complete forming the log. When finished, generously frost with the remaining whipped cream. Chill anywhere from 4 to 6 hours. Top with your favorite garnish. Slice at a 45-degree angle to serve. Serves approximately 8 to 10.

DIANE'S SUNDOWN SUPPER BOURBON CAKE

Margo and her friend Diane served a number of "Sundown Suppers" at the Milwaukee Repertory Theater. Diane's cake is always a hit with this hungry group.

1 *yellow cake mix*
1 *small vanilla pudding*
3 *eggs, beaten*
¾ *cup oil*
1 *teaspoon ground nutmeg*
¾ *cup bourbon*

Cream Cheese Frosting
½ *cup butter, softened*
1 *8-ounce package cream cheese, softened*
1 *teaspoon pure vanilla extract*
1 *pound powdered sugar, sifted*

Preheat the oven to 350°F. Cook the cake according to the mix, add the other ingredients, and pour into a Bundt pan. Bake until a toothpick inserted in the center comes out clean.

Meanwhile, to make the frosting, cream the butter, cream cheese, and vanilla in a large bowl until well blended. Add the powdered sugar gradually. Beat vigorously to a spreading consistency. If the frosting is too thick, thin it out with some milk. Frost the cake after it is done baking.

JEFF'S CRANBERRY
BIRTHDAY CAKE

Carol's family often prepares this cake for birthdays and other special occasions. Carol suggests doubling the sauce recipe.

1½ *teaspoons butter, softened and creamed*
½ *cup white sugar*
½ *cup milk*
1 *cup unsifted white flour*
1½ *teaspoon baking powder*
1 *package cranberries, washed and picked over*

Sauce
1 *stick butter*
¼ *cup cream*
½ *cup white sugar*
1 *teaspoon vanilla*

Preheat the oven to 350°F. In a large mixing bowl, thoroughly combine the butter, sugar, and milk. Mix the flour and baking powder together and add to the other mixture. Add the cranberries and combine. Pour into a greased 9 by 11-inch baking pan. Bake for 30 minutes, or until golden brown.

Meanwhile, to make the sauce, combine the butter, cream, and sugar in a saucepan. Boil for 5 minutes, or until thickened, stirring constantly and being careful that the mixture does not boil over. Remove from the heat. Add the vanilla and stir together. Pour over the cake and serve.

Carol's grandmother, Mary Bauer Davidson, wife of William A. Davidson, in her beloved garden at Pine Lake.

GRANDMOTHER WHYTE'S
EASY COFFEE CAKE

This recipe comes from Aunt Helen and Ellen's cookbook and was contributed by Ellen's Grandmother Whyte, mother of Malcolm Whyte, one of the founding attorneys of Whyte Hirschboeck Dudek S.C. in Milwaukee.

Around 1933, Mrs. Malcolm Whyte formed the Layton Art League to provide financial assistance for the art school with the ultimate goal of funding a new building. Because of the tireless work of the Layton School of Art Board President, Malcolm Whyte, her husband, the school became known as one of the top five art schools in the country. Layton School of Art has since merged with Milwaukee School of Art and Design.

Streusel Topping
1 *cup sugar*
3 *teaspoons cinnamon*
½ *cup flour*
¼ *cup melted butter*

Batter
¼ *cup butter*
1 *cup sugar*
2 *egg yolks*
1½ *cups flour*
4 *teaspoons baking powder*
½ *teaspoon salt*
2 *egg whites*
½ *cup milk*
½ *teaspoon vanilla or 1 teaspoon*
       lemon extract

To make the streusel topping, blend all of the ingredients together with a fork until the texture is crumbly.

To make the batter, cream the butter and add the sugar gradually. Cream well. Add the egg yolks and beat thoroughly. Sift the flour, measure, and resift with the baking powder and salt. Add to the creamed mixture, alternating with the milk.

Preheat the oven to 350°F. Beat the egg whites until stiff and fold into the creamed mixture. Add the vanilla. Mix well. Pour into a greased 7½ by 11½ by 1½-inch pan. (*Note:* This size pan may not exist any longer, but a pan similar in size will work.) Cover with the streusel topping. Bake for 25 minutes. This may be prepared in advance and refrigerated overnight, then baked in the morning.

BANANA BREAD

½ cup honey
1 teaspoon vanilla
1 cup mashed bananas
½ cup milk
½ cup butter
2 eggs
2 cups flour
¼ teaspoon salt
½ teaspoon baking soda

Cream Cheese Frosting
½ cup butter, softened
1 8-ounce package cream cheese, softened
1 teaspoon pure vanilla extract
1 pound powdered sugar, sifted

Preheat the oven to 350°F. Combine the honey, vanilla, bananas, and milk. Blend well and set aside. Cream the butter and eggs. Add the banana mixture and mix thoroughly. Combine the flour, salt, and baking soda. Slowly add the flour mixture, a small portion at a time, to the banana mixture, mixing thoroughly until all is combined. Pour into a greased loaf pan. Bake for 40 minutes. Do not overcook or the bread will be dry.

Meanwhile, to make the frosting, cream the butter, cream cheese, and vanilla in large bowl until well blended. Add the powdered sugar gradually. Beat vigorously to a spreading consistency. If the frosting is too thick, thin it out with some milk. Frost the cake after it's done cooking.

FAIRY FOOD

As a child, Carol liked to spend time with her Aunt Helen. This recipe was part of the fun.

1 cup white sugar
1 cup dark corn syrup

1 tablespoon white vinegar
1 tablespoon baking soda

Combine the sugar, syrup, and vinegar in a heavy pan. Cook over medium heat, stirring until the sugar dissolves. Continue cooking without stirring until brittle, or 300°F on a candy thermometer. Remove from the heat and quickly stir in the baking soda and mix well. Pour into a buttered square pan. Do not spread. Cool and brake into pieces. Makes about 1 pound.

Carol's grandparents, William A. Davidson and Mary Bauer Davidson, dressed in their Sunday best.

From the left: Mrs. Walter Davidson (Emma) with Jim McGee and Carol's mom, Marion "Midge" Davidson.

ZUCCHINI COOKIES

¾ cup oil
1½ cups honey
2 eggs, beaten
2 cups grated peeled zucchini
4 cups flour
1 tablespoon baking soda

3 tablespoons ground cinnamon
1 tablespoon ground nutmeg
1 tablespoon ground cloves
1 teaspoon salt
1 cup walnuts, chopped (optional)
2 cups raisins (optional)

In a medium-sized bowl, cream together the oil and honey until smooth. Add in the egg, then stir in the zucchini. Combine the flour, baking soda, cinnamon, nutmeg, cloves, and salt. Mix well. Add the zucchini mixture and blend well. Add the walnuts and raisins. Cover the dough and chill for at least overnight.

Preheat the oven to 375°F. Grease a cookie sheet. Drop the dough by teaspoonfuls spaced about 2 inches apart onto the cookie sheet.

Bake for 8 to 10 minutes, or until golden brown. Cool slightly on the cookie sheets before transferring to wire racks.

CHOCOLATE PEANUT BUTTER BARS

2 sticks butter, melted
1½ cups graham cracker crumbs
1 box powdered sugar
1 cup peanut butter

2 tablespoons shortening
1 12-ounce package semisweet
  chocolate morsels

Combine the butter, graham cracker crumbs, powdered sugar, and peanut butter. Press into a 9 by 13-inch pan. In a saucepan, mix together the shortening and chocolate morsels over low heat. Stir constantly until melted and smooth. Pour over the graham cracker mixture and spread evenly. Refrigerate before cutting into squares. *Hint:* To serve, take out of the refrigerator and let sit for 15 minutes before cutting.

RICOTTA CAKE
WITH FRESH BLUEBERRY TOPPING

Did you know that bears like blueberries? When blueberries are in season during the summer months, bears, with their acute sense of smell, will travel miles in order to feast on succulent blueberries.

Native Americans called blueberries "star berries" because the blossom at each end of the berry resembles a star. They harvested blueberries and smoked and dried them for later use. Native Americans combined preserved blueberries with cornmeal, honey, and water into the consistency of pudding.

Early settlers in North America used the fruit as an ingredient in foods and medicines. Blueberries became a staple in many early recipes. After being picked fresh off the bush, blueberries were used in soups, stews, and baked goods.

North America leads the world for blueberry production. July is National Blueberry Month. Blueberry muffins, pancakes, waffles, and pies are all American favorites.

Blueberry Topping
2½ *cups blueberries*
1 *teaspoon lemon juice*
½ cup sugar
½ cup water

Cake
½ cup ricotta cheese
2 *cups sugar*
1 *cup butter, softened*
½ cup milk
4 *eggs, slightly beaten*
1½ *teaspoons lemon extract*
Finely chopped zest of 1 lemon
3 *cups flour, sifted*
Powdered sugar

To prepare the topping, combine the blueberries, lemon juice, sugar, and water in a saucepan. Cook until thickened. Remove and cool.

To make the cake, preheat the oven to 350°F. Combine the ricotta, sugar, and butter and set aside. With a wire whisk, combine the milk, eggs, lemon extract, and lemon zest. Combine the flour and sugar. Add to the egg mixture and mix well. Pour into a 9 by 13-inch greased pan. Spoon the ricotta mixture over the egg mixture. Bake for 60 to 65 minutes. Cool on a rack. Dust lightly with powdered sugar. Serve a small slice with a spoonful of blueberry topping.

A handsome portrait of William James Harley and Rosemarie Muth Harley. Upon graduating from Washington High School, William took his first job at the Harley-Davidson factory working in the boiler room. After graduating from the University of Wisconsin in 1935 with a degree in mechanical engineering, Uncle Bill advanced to the Engineering Department, which was headed by his father. Margo's Uncle Bill rode his motorcycle to the factory for thirty years.

Margo's parents, Ann Harley and Charles Kohl, clown around for the camera. They married in 1941, and Margo's dad enlisted in World War II in an armored tank division.

MEXICAN WEDDING CAKES

These cakes can be made for Christmas. They freeze very well and the recipe can be doubled or tripled very easily.

1 *cup butter*
½ cup powdered sugar
½ teaspoon vanilla

½ cup pecans, chopped
½ teaspoon salt
1¾ *cups flour*

Preheat the oven to 350°F. Cream the butter and powdered sugar. Add the vanilla, pecans, salt, and flour. Shape into 1-inch balls and bake for 15 minutes. Let cool to the touch and immediately roll in powdered sugar. Cool completely and roll in sugar a second time.

APPLES WITH AMARETTO

Carol came up with this refreshing summer treat.

8 *crisp apples, peeled and thinly sliced (about ⅔ of an apple per person)*

1 *cup or more amaretto (or substitute any sweet liquor you like)*

Marinate the apple slices in enough amaretto to cover overnight and all of the next day. One hour before serving, remove the apples and arrange on a freezeproof tray and put in the freezer. To serve, put toothpicks into the apple slices and arrange on a platter. The slices will thaw as your guests nibble on them. Serves 10.

CAKE FOR THE ANGELS

This recipe is from an eighty-seven-year-old friend of Carol's from Kewanee, Wisconsin. Be sure to use slivered almonds, which don't have skins on them.

2 *tablespoons gelatin*
2 *cups cold milk*
4 *egg yolks*
1 *cup powdered sugar*
1 *teaspoon vanilla*
⅛ *teaspoon salt*

1 *pint real whipping cream*
1 *angel food cake (either bought or baked from package mix)*
1 *6-ounce package slivered almonds, toasted*

In a double boiler, combine the gelatin and cold milk. Heat and stir until dissolved. Let stand until lukewarm. In a mixing bowl, beat the egg yolks. Add the sugar, vanilla, and salt and stir. Add this mixture to the milk mixture. Let this stand until it just begins to thicken. Stir. In a mixing bowl, beat the whipping cream until it forms peaks. Add the milk mixture, folding in thoroughly. Ice the entire cake. Just before serving, cover the top with the toasted slivered almonds. In the old days, when eggs were cheap, this delicious cake cost only $1. Enjoy!

Baby Carol, granddaughter of William A. Davidson. This picture was taken in 1936, and you can see that she is a playful child.

Many birthdays to celebrate. Margo, right, her sister Kathleen, center, and friends honor another one with a canopied cake.

WACKY CAKE

1½ cups flour
3 tablespoons cocoa
1 cup sugar
1 teaspoon baking soda
½ teaspoon salt

5 tablespoons salad oil
1 teaspoon vinegar
1 teaspoon vanilla
1 cup cold water

Preheat the oven to 375°F. Sift the flour into a 9 by 9-inch cake pan. Add the cocoa, sugar, baking soda, and salt. Combine and make three holes in the mixture. Combine the salad oil, vinegar, and vanilla. Add to the flour mixture. To that, add the water and mix well. Bake for 25 minutes.

ESTELLE'S CHOCOLATE CAKE

2⅔ cups flour
6 tablespoons cocoa
2 teaspoons salt
2 teaspoons baking soda
2 teaspoons vanilla

2 tablespoons vinegar
2 cups sugar
1 cup oil
2 cups water

Preheat the oven to 350°F. Mix all of the ingredients together to form a batter. The batter will be very watery, but that's okay. Pour into a greased 9 by 13-inch pan. Bake for 30 to 40 minutes. Do not overbake.

FUDGE ON YOUR BIKE

This delicious treat comes to us from Carol's friend Ditty.

2 *cups heavy cream*
12 *ounces bittersweet or*
   semisweet chocolate pieces

4 *egg yolks, beaten*
1 *teaspoon vanilla*
3 *tablespoons butter, softened*

Heat the cream until almost boiling. Remove from the heat. Slowly add the chocolate pieces, stirring constantly. Slowly add the beaten egg yolks and stir. Add the vanilla and butter. Stir until thoroughly blended. Spoon into a shallow dish. Refrigerate until ready to serve.

NORTH CAROLINA FUDGE PIE

Carol's friend Ruth and her Southern relatives contributed this one.

¾ *cup butter or margarine, melted*
1½ *cups sugar*
½ *teaspoon vanilla*
3 *large eggs, lightly beaten*
⅓ *cup flour*

⅓ *cup cocoa*
¾ *cup chopped pecans*
1 *unbaked 9-inch pastry shell*
Vanilla ice cream (optional)

Preheat the oven to 350°F. Cream the butter and sugar. Blend in the vanilla. Add the eggs and mix well. Combine the flour, cocoa, and pecans. In thirds, add the flour mixture to the butter mixture, stirring well. Pour into the pastry shell. Bake for 35 to 40 minutes, or until set. Serve with ice cream. Yummy!

In 1950, Carol, right, and her friend Mimi, left, celebrate a birthday with a very fallen cake! This picture was taken at Ferry Hall in Lake Forest, Illinois, where Carol was a student. Carol's aunt Helen Davidson also graduated from Ferry Hall.

Baby Margo and her godfather, Arthur Harley Davidson, Jr. The Arthur Davidson family home was a short distance from the Harley home on Washington Boulevard. Arthur admitted that he spent more time at the Harley home than his own. Well, of course you need to realize that Art and John Harley were best friends! Art is second generation Davidson and definitely someone we all look up to with the utmost respect and reverence.

DIED-AND-GONE-TO-HEAVEN DESSERT

1 *cup flour*
1 *cup pecans, finely chopped*
1 *cube low-fat margarine*
1 *8-ounce package cream cheese*
1 *cup powdered sugar*
1 *large container whipped topping*
1 *small box instant vanilla pudding*

1 *small box instant chocolate pudding*
3 *cups low-fat milk*
2 *to* **3** *bananas, sliced*
1 *small container of whipped topping*
Toasted slivered almonds

Preheat the oven to 350°F. Cream the flour, pecans, and margarine to form the crust. Pat the crust into a 9 by 13-inch baking pan. Bake for 20 to 25 minutes, or until golden brown. Cool.

Cream the cream cheese and sugar together. Fold in the whipped topping and blend well. Spread onto the cooled baked crust.

Prepare the pudding with the milk. Layer half of the pudding into the pan. Add the bananas and top with the remaining pudding. Top with the whipped topping. Refrigerate overnight. Just before serving, sprinkle with toasted almonds.

BREAD PUDDING WITH RUM SAUCE

Rum or Whiskey Sauce
½ *cup butter*
1 *cup sugar*
1 *teaspoon vanilla*
1 *egg, beaten*
¼ *cup rum or whiskey*

Bread Pudding
1 *loaf day-old French bread, cubed*
1 *quart milk*
3 *eggs, well beaten*
2 *cups sugar*
2 *tablespoons vanilla extract*
1½ *tablespoons butter, melted*
2 *cups frozen berries of your choice (blueberries, raspberries, or blackberries)*

To make the sauce, cream together the butter and sugar in a medium-sized bowl. Add the vanilla. Slowly stir in the beaten egg. Add the rum or whiskey and blend well. Stir over low heat for 5 minutes. Set aside.

To make the bread pudding, in a large bowl, soak bread in the milk for about 30 minutes.

Preheat the oven to 350°F. In a bowl, mix together the eggs, sugar, and vanilla. Add the bread and mix together. Spread the melted butter over the bottom of a 9 by 13-inch baking pan. Add the bread mixture. Add the berries on top of the bread mixture, gently nudging them into the bread mixture. Bake, uncovered, for 30 minutes, or until bubbly hot. Remove from the oven. Place a generous serving on a plate and spoon the sauce over the top.

This is one of Margo's favorite pictures, a portrait of Margo and her mother, Ann Harley.

Carol raises her glass and toasts the memory of her mother.

MIDGE DAVIDSON'S
FAMOUS PEANUT BRITTLE

Carol's mom, Marion "Midge" Davidson, was known for her peanut brittle.

1 *cup water*
2 *cups sugar*
1 *cup corn syrup*
2 *cups raw unsalted Spanish peanuts*

1 *teaspoon salt*
1 *to* **3** *tablespoons butter*
¼ *teaspoon baking soda*
1 *teaspoon vanilla*

In a large saucepan, bring the water to a boil. Remove from the heat and stir in the sugar until dissolved. Add the corn syrup and blend well. Cook to the hard-boil stage, or 250°F on a candy thermometer. Immediately add the peanuts. Stir. Cook barely to the hard-crack stage, or 295°F. Gently blend in the butter, baking soda, and vanilla. *Important:* Be careful not to burn the candy mixture.

Pour onto a buttered slab. Quickly spread the mixture. Loosen the mixture and flip it over. Begin to pull the brittle thin and even. When cool, crack it into bite-sized pieces. Line a tin with wax paper and layer the brittle in between layers of wax paper. Cover tightly, as moisture will cause the brittle to stick together.

Zen and the Art of Motorcycle Mixology

The mixed drink, or cocktail, has long been associated with the start of the twentieth century. The cocktail became a more interesting concoction than plain beer or whiskey. The cocktail was an invention-in-progress.

And, with inventions such as the automobile, motorcycle, and new farming implements, the ordinary citizen was experiencing the luxury of more leisure time. The cocktail became fun and popular!

THE SIDECAR

The beginning of the twentieth century has long been considered to be the "golden age" of cocktails. However, the origin of the cocktail is believed to date all the way back to the early 1800s. The term *cocktail* was first seen in the American magazine *The Balance* in the May 13, 1806, issue, stating, "Cocktail is a stimulating liquor, composed of spirits of any kind, sugar, water, and bitters—it is vulgarly called bittered sling and is supposed to be an excellent electioneering potion."

The sidecar cocktail was invented at the legendary Harry's New York Bar in Paris during World War I. The bar was founded in 1911 and became a favorite watering hole of the rich and famous, including Ernest Hemingway, F. Scott Fitzgerald, Toscanini, Charlie Chaplin, Truman Capote, Orson Welles, Aristotle Onassis, Peggy Guggenheim, and Woody Allen.

As the story goes, the cocktail was named after an eccentric army captain who insisted on being chauffeur-driven to the bar in a motorcycle sidecar. The sidecar remains one of the most prominent drinks of the twentieth century.

The very first time Margo was served a sidecar was when her dear friend Bob, an excellent mixologist, made an entire pitcher of them, as is his way. They were delicious, every last one! Here is Bob's recipe.

Lemon slices
Bar sugar or simple syrup (to frost
   the glasses)
⅔ part cognac

⅓ part Cointreau
Juice of 1 lemon
Lemon twists

First, rub a lemon slice around the edge of a martini glass, then dip the glass in a saucer of bar sugar. Fill a cocktail shaker with ice and pour in the liquid ingredients. Shake. Pour into the glass. Garnish with a lemon twist. Enjoy!

Opposite page: A 1918 drawing of patent number 1,301,257, a sidecar body that William S. Harley, Chief Engineer of the Harley-Davidson Motor Company, invented. The improvements were such that the new design of the sidecar allowed it to be nested, making shipping and storage more cost-effective.

SIDE CAR BODY AND METHOD OF PACKING THE SAME.
APPLICATION FILED SEPT. 13, 1918.

1,301,257.

Patented Apr. 22, 1919.

2 SHEETS—SHEET 1.

Fig. 1.

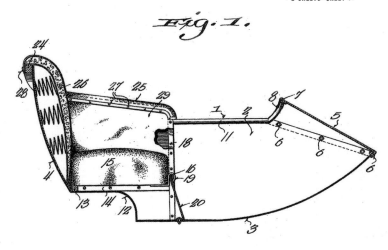

Fig. 2.

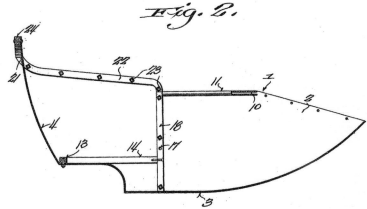

WITNESSES:

INVENTOR

William S. Harley

BY

141

W. S. HARLEY.

SIDE CAR FOR MOTOR CYCLES.

APPLICATION FILED AUG. 20, 1915.

1,212,350.

Patented Jan. 16, 1917.

4 SHEETS—SHEET 2.

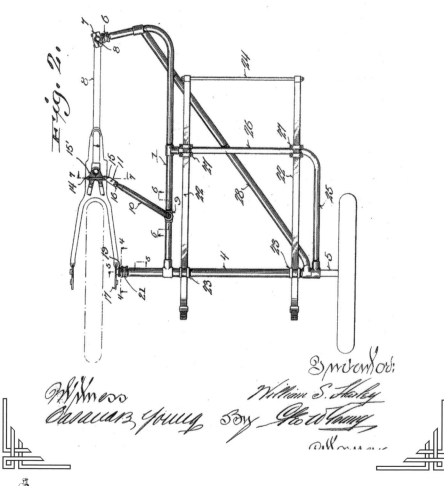

Fig. 2.

Witness:

Inventor:

William S. Harley

By

AFTER-THE-RIDE PUNCH

2 *cups Southern Comfort bourbon*
2 *cups fresh orange juice*
¼ *cup fresh lemon juice*

2 *quarts dry champagne*
2 *dashes of angostura bitters*

Mix the Southern Comfort and orange and lemon juices over ice. Add the champagne and bitters. Pour into glasses and enjoy!

BLUE MOTORCYCLE

Equal parts gin, vodka, light rum,
  blue curaçao, and Triple Sec

Splash of sour mix
Lemon-lime soda

In a shaker over ice, mix the gin, vodka, rum, blue curaçao, Triple Sec, and sour mix. Shake for a few seconds. Pour into glasses and fill with lemon-lime soda.

THE BIG V

Equal parts grenadine, white crème de cacao, and blue curaçao

Pour the grenadine into a shot glass. Pour the white crème de cacao into the glass over a spoon, and then pour the blue curaçao in the same manner. This cocktail will look red, white, and blue if it is made properly!

Opposite page: A 1915 drawing of patent number 1,212,350, a sidecar for motorcycles that William S. Harley, Chief Engineer of the Harley-Davidson Motor Company, invented. This invention designs an unprecedented form of coupling that enabled the sidecar to be attached or detached from the body of the motorcycle. More importantly, as William S. wrote, "the primary aim of this invention is to produce a coupling for sidecars of motorcycles by means of which all strains or the like incidental to the starting of the motorcycle are so distributed that they are reduced to the minimum; and also to produce a coupling in which the shocks, jars, and other vibrations incidental to the movement of the motorcycle and car are not transmitted from one to another."

AMERICAN FLAG

½ ounce each vodka, rum, tequila,
  gin, and blue curaçao

2 ounces sour mix
2 ounces lemon-lime soda

In a shaker over ice, add the vodka, rum, tequila, gin, blue curaçao, and sour mix. Shake for a few seconds. Fill a tall glass with ice cubes. Pour the contents from the shaker into the glass. Add lemon-lime soda and stir gently.

HANDLEBAR

1½ ounces good Scotch
½ Rose's Lime Juice

¾ ounce Drambuie

In a shaker over ice, add all of the ingredients. Shake for a few seconds. Strain and serve this cocktail straight up.

Opposite page: A 1917 drawing of a patent number 1,262,787, a shock-absorber for handlebars that William S. Harley, Chief Engineer of the Harley-Davidson Motor Company, invented. This invention designs a resilient shock-absorbing connection between the handgrips and the handlebar proper. This invention accommodated the handlebars currently in use and those yet to be produced, resulting in a savings for the company.

SHOCK ABSORBER FOR HANDLE BARS.
APPLICATION FILED OCT. 15, 1917.

1,262,787.

Patented Apr. 16, 1918.

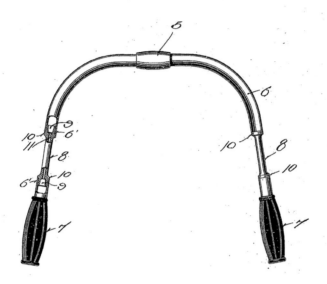

Inventor:
William S Harley
By Geo W Young
Attorneys

Witness:

145

CAROL'S FAVORITE SPICED RUSSIAN TEA

This is especially good if you get a cold or after a ride—or just on any cold and wintry day.

2 *cups Tang or similar powdered drink*
½ *cup instant tea with no sugar or lemon added*
½ *cup sugar*

1 *8-ounce package lemonade mix*
1 *teaspoon ground cloves*
1 *teaspoon ground allspice*
1½ *teaspoons ground cinnamon*

Mix all of the ingredients together and store in a tightly covered jar until needed. To use, put 2 to 3 tablespoons in a cup or mug and pour boiling water over and stir.

KAHULA-HALOOA

This cocktail is perfect for sitting by the campfire after dinner.

4 *cups sugar*
4¼ *cups water*
¾ *cup instant coffee*

1 *fifth vodka*
1 *vanilla bean, chopped*

Mix together the sugar and 4 cups of the water and boil for approximately 10 minutes. Heat the coffee and the remaining ¼ cup water until just before it boils. Let cool. Mix both liquids together. Add the fifth of vodka. Divide into 2 clean bottles. Divide the vanilla bean between the 2 bottles. Store for 3 weeks, shaking once every other day. After that, strain the liquid with a cheesecloth. Be careful—this drink is strong!

As the company continued to develop and mature, so did the buildings. The company definitely was a work in progress. Very few companies share this simple story of success. From the onset, Harley-Davidson has weathered definite ups and downs. Any business does. However, for whatever reasons, there is a mystique, a loyalty, a following, that propels the company forward. Carol and Margo have participated in 100th Anniversary events—Margo in the Harley ancestral home in Littleport, England, and Carol in Barcelona, Spain. Above, in front of an expanding factory, are the founders with part of their team: Walter Davidson, second from the left; Arthur Davidson, fourth from the left; William A. Davidson, second from the right; and William S. Harley, far right.

About the Authors

Margo Manning is the granddaughter of William Sylvester and Anna Caroline Harley. Her mother is their only daughter, Ann. William S. Harley always encouraged his children to make their own way—just as he did. Margo followed in her mother's footsteps and made her career in the arts. She began by teaching art in a correctional facility and moved on to work in the performing arts. Currently, Margo is Associate Director of Development at the Milwaukee Repertory Theater. She lives in Milwaukee with her trusted companions, Jack, Bobby, and Minnie.

Carol Lange is the granddaughter of William and Mary Bauer Davidson. Her parents were Marion Davidson and Frederick Lange, Jr. She is their only child. Art and antiques have always been her main interests. She worked at the Milwaukee Art Center with Ann Harley Kohl (Margo's mom). Later Carol had her own antique shop, which specialized in majolica pottery, in California. An earthquake forced her to close her shop, after which she went into the travel consulting business. Carol has lived in the same house in Los Gatos, California, for twenty-nine years. She has two sons—John, an attorney who lives with his family in Milwaukee, and Jeff, a pilot for American Airlines who lives in Fresno.

Acknowledgments

Carol and Margo would like to thank friends and family who took the time to contribute their kitchen-tested specialties or pass on those treasured recipes that have been handed down from their mothers: Marion "Midge" Davidson and Ann Harley; grandmothers Mary Bauer Davidson and Anna Jachthuber Harley; and Margo's great-grandmother Mary Smith Harley. Thanks to all of you, especially: Margo's cousins, Hans and Brigitte Jachthuber from Straubing, Germany; Carol's children, their wives, and grandchild—Jeff and Evy, and John, Mary, and baby Sam; friends—Maja Jurisic and Don Fraker, Katie Rynkiewicz, Donna Dollase, Diane Dalton, Charlotte and George Mabry, Josephine Simpson, and Robert Bodus; Margo's stepmother, Hazel Kohl; and everyone else, thank you! To Jack, Bobby, and Minnie: thank you for your love and understanding; we'll get out on the road again soon now that the writing is done.

Carol and Margo would also like to thank Kate Hawley, our designer, who kept us on the right road while finishing our book. Kate, in turn, introduced us to Pamela Scesniak, a most inventive illustrator, who brought life to four very important scenes in our memory of the four founders of Harley-Davidson Motor Company.

This book would not be possible without the contributions of Harley family members John and Kate Harley, and Mary Harley Stocking, who culled precious photos from their family archives for use in the book. Mike Gallagher, from Door County, was an invaluable resource regarding the Harley and Davidson families. Our very special thanks to you all!

Finally, we also pay homage to two of the best cooks and editors of the first family recipe collection: Helen Davidson Morton and Ellen Whyte Stolz. Thank you for your creativity, enthusiasm, and inventiveness!